MISERY
TO
Ministry

MISERY

TO

Ministry

MISERY TO MINISTRY PUBLICATIONS

Misery to Ministry
Copyright © 2010 by Mary T. Sorrendino

ISBN 978-0-9749664-9-6

Published by:
Misery To Ministry Publications
Syracuse, NY

Some of the names have been changed in this autobiography.

This book is dedicated to:
God
Because without Him
this book would never have been written.
I owe Him everything.
He is my everything.

CONTENTS

FOREWORD

Who am I? It was not that bad. There were no bruises, and therefore it was not too bad. I know that others had it much worse. Everybody has something to overcome. I was convinced that my experience was not that unique. However, the older I got the more convinced I became that by the grace of my God I overcame the **lies**.

The lies: what were they? We all have some lies. All children go through the awkward stage. All young adolescents ask, "Who am I?" What is it that makes me think that I have to share my experience? The answer is that by God's grace and His intervention I was able to overcome the psychological abuse, the fear, and the oppression of the crippling shame that I carried with me.

PART I
The Early Years - Downstate

▌·knew she was gone. The moment I saw the mail in the ▌ : mailbox, I knew . . . she had not checked her mail today, or ▌ the day before. As I walked down the driveway towards the back door, I knew. She always got her mail. Her paranoid mind would not allow her to neglect it, not for one day . . . .

Gary sensed my concern and walked with me to the back door. Craig and Stacy, Gary's two children, waited in the car. I entered through the back porch and then through the swinging door. To my right I saw her leg. I then said out loud to Gary what I already knew in my heart: "She's dead." Gary went over to her to feel for a pulse in her neck. Her eyes were open and very black. She was 63 years old. I was 33.

* * * *

We were more than Mom could handle. Not having a clue that there would be two of us, she couldn't have imagined the overwhelming responsibility of having twins. Our brother John was three and a half. She was hoping to have a daughter, a confidante, someone to be her friend. We were due in October, but we arrived on August 5, 1956 in Manhattan, New York in Doctors' Hospital. She got two for one—good for bragging rights—and Dad got drunk.

The Bronx

I have few memories from the Bronx.

"Mary, would you please get me a beer?" he always asked. I was just three years old when we lived in the Bronx.

"Yes." I walk to the refrigerator and I hope that I can have a sip. Mom opens the bottle of Ballantine beer. I am very careful not to spill it.

"Thank you, sweetie."

"Can I please have a sip?"

"Yes."

I sip the beer and it is cold, and I like the taste. He always says yes, but I must ask and use my manners. Sure I liked the taste! I acquired it when I was very young. Mom told me that Dad would give Toni and me beer in our bottles to stop us from crying.

While in the Bronx, I remember having a friend who lived next door to us. I do not remember her name but I know that when Toni and I were with her we had fun. Unfortunately, her older brother was cruel; he was constantly scaring Toni and me. One time he took our stick horses and stuck them in the bushes and another time he had on a Halloween mask and I was afraid. Although this time was short lived, I remember the relief I felt when I knew that we were going to move away from him.

It's moving day, and I am about 3½ years old. I lie in bed staring at the blue nightlight, which illuminates the Virgin Mary's picture. It's quiet and I know that today is the big day. The moving van is packed and we get into our black 1958 Chevy. As we drive away, Toni and I look out of the back window of the car; we see our friend as she chases us. She's crying, "Don't leave!!!" I feel really bad for her.

We arrived in Plainview, Long Island, 29 Relda Street. Mom pointed out that we had the biggest house on the block. It was pink and it had a bay window that went from the floor to the ceiling. Although it was a ranch-style home, its appearance was different from any other on the block. Mom was extremely excited about the house, and she mentioned that they had built it. I didn't understand what she was talking about, but it looked nice.

★ ★ ★ ★

Mom was a beautiful lady, though she was not very tall. She stood about 5' ½" and weighed about 110 lbs. Her natural curls were exceptionally beautiful. She had small, sweetheart lips. Her mom and dad were born in Italy; therefore Mom was the first generation born in the USA. Her father was Sicilian and her mother Calabrian. Mom was the third daughter, followed by six brothers, all born in Syracuse, New York. She was named Julia Prince. She claimed that she didn't have a middle name, though I found out years later it was Eleanor, after her "cumae," which means godmother in Italian. Although her name was Julia, she was often called Judy.

She was a vivacious lady who loved life. At age 22 she decided to make a big move to New York City, and she did it. After having her first marriage annulled, she was free. She went to the big city and met a Jewish man named John. They married and had a son named John, but that marriage did not last. Eventually she met Harry L. Haupt. She was struck with his good looks and they married in August 1955.

My father Harry was strikingly handsome. He was 5' 8" and weighed about 160 lbs. He had beautiful, thick black hair that he combed back in a wave, like Elvis. He was dark complexioned, and he looked Native American though he was just ¼ Cherokee as well as ¼ German and ½ Irish. His paternal grandmother was full-blooded Cherokee and his grandfather full-blooded German. Mom would say that Dad looked like a movie star. Well, he did. He worked with the movie stars in New York City at 20th Century Fox. He was a grip man. I also heard him say that he was the best boy. Later I learned that he was a key grip and worked dolly grip as well. He made great money for 1958 and was able to build a home on Long Island.

My father grew up in Harlem, New York City, and he was the youngest of four sons. My father had a lot of grief in his life. The first tragedy was the death of his brother Jim. Jim was 21 years old when he died, and that loss was very difficult for my father.

My father was patriotic, and when Pearl Harbor was bombed on December 7, 1941, the day before his 15th birthday, my father, a middle school dropout, made the decision to enlist. I was told that two years later, on December 8, 1943, he lied about his age and joined the Navy at age 17. He was a veteran of both WWII and the Korean War. He received a purple heart because his ship blew up. I was told that only three men survived and one of them was my dad. His fingers were blown off and reattached.

Dad had some real problems: he had a traumatic history from his military experiences, unresolved grief issues, and two failed marriages just like my mom. I did not know for years, but he was tormented by the fact that he was not a father to his two daughters from his second marriage, Penny and Marsha. They lived with their mom. Dad's biggest problem was that he was a drinker. Not only did he drink, he was a mean drunk! He would fight with the neighbors and it was embarrassing. Of course he fought with my mom as well.

It is strange; so often society does not realize that dysfunction extends across social and economic classes. My parents had money, looks, and status. Nonetheless, those things could not prevent the madness or the drinking, and nothing could stop the hell we lived in.

∗ ∗ ∗ ∗

I can't remember when there was a peaceful environment. I recall John being in trouble all of the time. I truly felt sorry for him—Mom yelling at him, chasing him with the broom. I thought of the cartoon where the cat was chasing the mouse. John would often act out and our mom would RAGE!

John would say, "I WILL BE GOOD."

My mom would mock his plea: **"I will be good, I will be good."** She never believed him.

I didn't know that my brother John had a different father than Toni and I. I was only aware that he was my big brother and that Mom said he was **BAD.**

When we moved to Long Island we were almost four years old, but Mom and Dad still had us in our cribs. Toni's was on one side of the room and mine was on the other. There wasn't much space between us: if we stretched with all our might we could grab each other's hands. Toni would stretch her hands to mine, and then we would use all of our strength and pull our cribs next to each other's. That way one of us could climb into the other crib. Soon I was able to get out of my crib, and I would stand next to Toni's crib and coax her to get out. I told her I would catch her if she fell. I was the risk taker.

Toni and I were very close, and being identical twins allowed us always to have someone we could count on. I am truly grateful to God for my twin; I don't think I could have survived without her.

Dad and Mom were often yelling. I pretended that I was asleep, because that way I wouldn't get spanked. When Dad came home Mom would tell him how bad I was; I was always "talking back," whatever that meant. I didn't understand, but whatever "talking back" was, I was in trouble for it. Toni was the "peacemaker," saying, "Mary, just be good. Don't say anything and it will be okay."

* * * *

When Toni and I were adults, we asked ourselves when it was that Mom turned against me. I said that I thought it was when I pushed Toni down the stairs. I did push her down the basement stairs, because I had seen it in a cartoon and it looked fun. The plan was that she would go first and then it would be my turn. Well . . . she went tumbling head over heals and she could have been killed. Mom was through the roof!!!! I thought it was then that she saw the evil in me.

Toni brought to my attention that when we were born she came home at 6 weeks old. She thinks that Mom began to bond with her. Then, 6 weeks later at 3 months old, I came home from the hospital and we were more than she could handle. I would cry and wake up Toni; I'm sure it was difficult. These were hard times for my mom, and she would throw them up in our faces: "I WAS UP WITH YOU TWO FOR A YEAR!!!" I cannot count the number of times I heard that statement. As I got older, I remember thinking *I never asked to be born*. It was not long before I would say those words to her.

* * * *

I was four years old when I learned that something was wrong with Toni and me: we were defective. The first thing we learned was that we had Indian straight hair. One thing John had was beautiful curls, just like Mom. Mom kept our hair short, pixy cut, and on occasion she would curl our hair with the use of perms. I hated the perms: they smelled bad and I didn't like the way I looked with the curls. Actually, I didn't like the way I looked period.

It's the day we are getting our hair cut. Mom does it in the living room, and she is loud and very angry. She starts with Toni and I can see that she is hurting her. "YOU HAVE SUCH BABY-FINE HAIR!! I CAN'T DO ANYTHING WITH IT!"

Toni sits still and is very quiet so Mom won't pull her hair any harder. It is obvious that Mom is very angry, and she continues with her tirade.

Now it is my turn .... Mom pulls my hair and it hurts; she yells at how fine it is: "I hate this Indian straight hair! It's baby fine and I can't do anything with it!! I don't know why you couldn't have my curls!!"

I keep very still as she rages. The more she cuts the angrier she gets. She says over and over again how baby fine it is and how she hates Indian straight hair!! With clenched fists she cries out, "Why, why couldn't you have curls like me?!!"

This was a constant battle every time she cut our hair, and it happened often because she had to keep it very short.

Strange Noises

Toni and I heard a strange noise coming from John's bedroom, and we went to check it out. We walked into John's room. Mom and Dad were there, and at first I didn't understand what was going on. John was on the bed with his arms stretched out, and I saw that his mouth was **gagged.** Then I realized that he was **tied down to the bed!!!** He looked so helpless and afraid. **I was horrified!**

Mom said, "We can't keep spanking him to make him mind!" She was justifying their corrective technique. I don't remember what we said, but that incident will forever be etched in my mind—his look of helplessness and the fear in his eyes.

Not long after that John, who was just 9 years old, was put into a mental institution. He had a "nervous breakdown." He was institutionalized at Kings Park Psychiatric Center in New York. Mom said, "When children **won't mind** they **have** to be put away."

With John out of the family, I then became the main target.

New Home New Baby

Mom was going to have a baby; Mom and Dad both wanted a boy to carry on the Haupt name. On April 4, 1960, Harry Lawrence Haupt, Jr. was born.

I couldn't wait to play with Harry. I imagined him crawling on a blanket on the floor. We loved him, and Toni and I couldn't wait for him to be big enough to play with. He was so tiny and beautiful. Mom said he was too small to play with.

Everywhere we went with him, strangers would comment on how beautiful he was. He also developed an outgoing personality. He would actually flirt with the cashiers. I was so proud of him and worried about him a lot.

I thank God that Mom taught us about God. She would read bedtime Bible stories. My favorite one was about Joseph and the colored coat. I was unable to comprehend how mean his brothers were to him. Mom told Toni and me about her brothers and how much she loved them. She told us how wonderful her brother was when he took the punishment for her. My mom was smoking a cigarette in the bathroom at her parents' house, and when her father smelled it he demanded to know who the culprit was. Before my mom could confess, her brother Joe said that it was him. My Uncle Joe, who was innocent, took the punishment for my mom.

I was impressed with the fact that her brother loved her so much. So at a young age I began to develop a strong bond with my siblings.

Mom sent us to Our Lady of Mercy Church. It was a long walk across a busy street but there was a light, so Mom let us go to church by ourselves. When Harry was about 5 and we were 8, she let us bring him to church. I was SO proud of him. This was MY BROTHER and everyone loved him! Who wouldn't? He had both looks and personality. I was always protective of him, afraid that he would be hurt. But there was no need to worry because Mom loved him and so did Dad.

Starting Elementary School

We began kindergarten at Fern Place Elementary School when we were 5, but we were very small for our age; we were probably the smallest kids in the class. Mom had to buy us special triple A shoes, and she bought us our school dresses from Saks Fifth Avenue. I knew that because she would always brag about where she shopped.

I did not want to go to school, and incidentally that became a constant for me. I was crying and carrying on to no avail. Toni seemed to like school. Every day we would sing and the teacher would play the piano. She would allow the children to take turns turning the music pages as she played. I never raised my hand. I didn't care about the music. Now, Toni loved it; she would always raise her hand and she was often picked to turn the pages. I don't think the teacher was playing favorites; I just didn't see a reason to raise my hand. I suspect most of my classmates agreed with me.

First Grade

In first grade, Toni and I were placed in different classes at school. My teacher favored me; she seemed to think I was special. Every day in class I had my own work. While everyone else had to copy five sentences from the blackboard, I only had two. My teacher would get a sheet of paper and write out two sentences just for me. She would have me complete these special assignments and I was done for the day! Great! I hated doing the work, and I liked the easier work and the attention.

One day Toni and I talked about switching classes just for the fun of it. Mom always dressed us identically, so we made plans to meet in the bathroom after lunch. After we met, I went into Toni's class and Toni went into mine.

I could not believe that Toni didn't have her desk next to the teacher like I did. Also, she had to do ALL of the work, just like the rest of the class!!

Toni was in my class and thought, *What is going on here? How come Mary has separate assignments?* We stayed in each other's classes until the end of the day. No one knew that we had changed classes.

Before we would go into the house after school, Toni would say, "Mary, just put your foot down and say "No yelling tonight!'" She would lift her leg and stamp her right foot on the sidewalk: "Come on Mary, do it. You do it and say '**No yelling tonight!!'**"

I would reluctantly agree and follow her instructions. I picked up my foot and slammed it on the sidewalk hard and said, "**No yelling tonight!**"

We entered the home and it wasn't long before Mom started

yelling about something. I said, "There's no use." I had given up.

Second Grade

I was having difficulty behaving both at home and in school. Despite the extra attention I received in first grade, I wasn't prepared for second grade. There were no special assignments **just for me.** I had to do all of the work just like the rest of the class, and it was overwhelming. The teacher didn't like me, and she constantly had to redirect me to the task at hand.

School was always difficult; I could never stay focused. *Everything is hard!* **I can't think** *and nothing makes sense.*

I was lazy and quite possibly stupid. The room seemed dark and the teacher was mean. Every day the homework assignment was on the blackboard. It was probably there all day, but I didn't copy it—maybe because I couldn't see all that well. But at the end of the day she would erase it and I had no idea what the assignment was. I was unwilling to ask for help. I had given up. *Nothing ever changes*, I thought. *Mom will* **always rage** *and* **he** *will always be drunk.* I would escape daily to my daydreams where I didn't have to face the truth that I was different than others. Toni seemed okay; she was smart. I just didn't care anymore—what was the point? *I'm stupid and I just don't care!* I was only 7 years old.

Dad was in charge while we lived in Long Island. There were times that he worked long hours at 20th Century Fox, and when he came home if we were still awake we had to run to bed and pretend to be asleep. Mom was nervous because she would be in trouble if we were awake.

Dad drank daily and regularly arrived home intoxicated.

Long Island School and Home Life

There was no refuge: second grade in school had become a nightmare and home was a night terror. One thing I believed was that **if** there were no such thing as **dinner,** life would be so much better. Dinner was the worst time of the day. We had to eat everything on our plates. Dad and Mom sat in the living room while Toni, Harry, and I sat in the kitchen.

During the sixties the TV families looked perfect; everyone ate dinner together and talked. At our home, dinner was a negative experience.

Dad says, "No talking in there!"

I'm holding back the laughter. I would always laugh. I don't know what was funny, but Harry would do something cute and I would laugh. Toni gives me that look of concern, which communicates the question, "Are you out of your mind???"

Then the ritual starts. I ask, "May I please be excused?"

Mom looks at my plate. "No, I worked hard to make that." (Sometimes she slides a little over to the side and says "Finish this much.")

We sit . . . .

I'm so full I can't even finish my milk, and I love milk. Sometimes we sit there until 7:00 at night when Dad says that we can't leave the table until we finish every bite!! A few times when I finished every bite I would vomit up the meal; it was just too much food for my little stomach.

Another day at school, and I wish I could hide. I don't want anyone to see me. I am unable to think and I feel disconnected. I am alone in the confusion that consumes me. I want to get connected, to be a part of the group, but it is as though everyone is talking another language and I am not welcome into their secret club. I am in second grade and I continue to struggle. I don't remember anything that was taught. As the teacher talked it was like the adults on Peanuts: "WAWA WAAWA." Staying focused was impossible, and I was always struggling with learning.

I had studied my spelling words, but they didn't stick in my head. It was the day before the spelling test, and the teacher must have told my parents that I was lazy and not working in class. I didn't know why Toni could spell; she worked hard at it and she did a great job. Toni said that she could remember the weekly spelling words, but she had a hard time when there were bigger tests.

Dad said, "Come on girls, I'm going to test you on your spelling."

I thought to myself, *Oh no, I can't do this! I'm so nervous.* Dad had my special paddle at his side. We all had special paddles: they were from our paddle toys with the long rubber band and the little ball at the end. When Mom bought the red one I thought, *Wow this is different.* It was thick and red, and definitely sturdier. I enjoyed hitting the ball; what I didn't know was that my dad would like it and decide to use it against me . . . .

Dad removed the rubber band and ball and he had the perfect paddle. Mine was the thick red one. Toni and Harry had the standard paddles; mine was the thickest because I was the baddest.

Dad says, "Spell 'friends.'"

I say, "Friends: F-R-E-I-N-D-S."

"NO!"

I jump as the paddle hits the coffee table.

Again he says, "Friends."

I am shaking: "F-R-E-I-N-D-S."

Again the paddle **slams** against the table. I don't know how long this goes on before he hits my butt with it. He is very angry that I don't know my spelling words. Toni watches helplessly; she wants to give me the answer, but she is so nervous that she can't think straight. It's no use. Nothing helps me to learn. He eventually whacks my butt with the paddle! It hurts and I don't want him to see the tears.

Telling the time was also difficult, and I am grateful that my mom helped me. Dad would ask us at random times what time it was. I was a mess, but I knew how to count by fives.

"Mom, what time is it?"

"6:35."

"6:35. Okay." *God, please let him ask me the time. PLEASE let him ask me.* I'm pacing in the kitchen, looking and praying that he'll ask me **now.** I know that it's now 6:40. *Oh God, please have him call me into the living room and ask me now when I can get it right.* I feel my heart racing. I need him to ask me now; it's 6:45.... He never asks, and now I have left the kitchen and forgotten about the time. I have other work to do ....

"Mary, what time is it?"

Oh my God, I don't know. Mom is nowhere around. I'm all alone and I have to figure it out, but it's so confusing; there are no numbers on the clock over the oven. I need help. My heart begins to race and I can't think! I'm crying and I can't see!!!! He calls again, "MARY, what is the time???"

As I enter the room, I say "7:30."

He shouts, "NO! Go look again."

My stomach is sick and I'm still crying. I HAVE AB-SOLUTELY NO IDEA WHAT TIME IT IS. It's like a foreign language; I don't understand how to tell time! I am stupid.

I come back and I guess again. I am anticipating the slam of my special paddle on the table. **Whack!!** I jump. I guess again and he slams the paddle. Fear is gripping me. He eventually hits me with the paddle.

Mom steps in and they begin to yell. She asks, "What are you doing?!"

Dad responds innocently, "I'm teaching her how to tell time!" He gets angry and says, "She's seven years old and can't tell time!!"

Mom, in a raised voice, says, "That's because you make it confusing!"

Dad defensively replies, "Oh yeah, I'M THE BAD GUY. I never know what you want from me! You tell me to correct them and then you yell at me!! I DON'T know what you want from me!!!!!"

They continued to yell and I was crying. I went to my room, and Mom came in and sat with Toni and me and taught us how to tell time that day. She had our old wind-up Fisher-Price clock and she taught us to cut the clock in half. She made it so simple that I was able to understand. Still, I always struggled reading the kitchen clock because it didn't have numbers; it had lines where the number should have been. I also had trouble seeing the clock because it was so small. I would ask Dad if I could see his watch so I could see the numbers.

The day my mom taught Toni and me to tell time is one of my best memories of her. I also think back to coming home from school and finding the house immaculate and a surprise on my dresser. Toni and I both received a gift. Those were the best days. Mom would say that we were good and somehow earned the surprise; the problem was that I didn't know what I had done that was different. Being bad all the time, it was difficult for me to tell the difference. One interesting thing that Mom would always say was that Toni was the good twin and I was the bad twin. She referred to a movie called *The Bad Seed* and said that I was the bad seed.

∗ ∗ ∗ ∗

Sometimes we would go to the shopping center. She would buy us each a gift, like a toy or some Colorforms, while we were out shopping. We had a good time, but somehow I would always get her angry and she would yell at me nonstop—I didn't know what I had done to set her off, but I knew this: I was BAD and in big trouble. If I had known what I did that was so bad, perhaps I could have stopped. She would yell, "Just wait until your father gets home." She would yell and yell. I often hid under John's bed with my new toy; I would try to block out the yelling and focus on my toy. I would pretend that all was well and no one knew where I was. (Although John was in the state hospital there was always a bed for John wherever we lived.)

Harry was three and half years younger than Toni and I, and we loved him very much. Dad favored him. Every Saturday they would play together, building model cars and then crashing them. After they destroyed the cars, they buried them on the side of the house.

Everything Harry did was cute. One day Mom bought us little wastebaskets for our bedrooms; later that night Dad came home and was in a good mood and gave us all a brand new one-dollar bill. Harry got so excited. He came running out of his bedroom saying, "Hurry, come look! I have something in my new basket." We all went in and saw a new one-dollar bill ripped in pieces. Mom saved it because she thought it was cute.

One thing for sure was that Harry was loved. I do believe that they loved Toni, too. Who wouldn't? She was kind and tried very hard to make Mommy happy. Then one day I figured out how I could gain her love. Oftentimes Mom would not be able to find the yellow can opener. It was a handheld bottle opener and can opener, and it had a magnet for putting it on the refrigerator when you were done opening a bottle or can. Well, Mom would **yell** when she couldn't find the opener; I mean, she would get into a **rage over it.** She would yell, "WHERE IS THE OPENER?!!! **WHO TOOK IT?"** I noticed that whoever found the opener would be given praise. Toni would help Mom find it and she would be so happy that she would say, "What a good girl you are, Toni. Thank you!!!" Mom was so happy.

So I had a plan: when Mom would get really angry with me, I would hide the can opener. Sooner or later she would be on the hunt for it. Well, when it happened I knew right where it was, so then I was the one to find it, and Mom was so very happy with me and said that I was a good girl.

It made me happy to hear her say that, but deep down I

knew that I had set the whole thing up. I thought, *When I didn't hide it she blamed us kids anyway, so why not hide it?* I was in trouble if I did it or not.

Visitors from Syracuse

My mother's family would visit us in Long Island. This was a time of reprieve for us; all we had to do was behave, and as long as we were good while the company was there all would be great. My cousins came and that was great to get to know them. Aunt Sally, my mom's sister, and Uncle Louie visited with their children, Louie and Kathy. Aunt Fay came with her two children, Toni and Jimmy, and a few others came at least once.

Uncle Joe and Aunt Bev came numerous times. We absolutely loved it when they would visit, because they would stay awhile and we just LOVED our cousin Jo Jo, who was two years younger than we were. My mom and dad would take them to New York City for an exciting night on the town. To make it easy, Uncle Joe brought along one of his neighbors from Syracuse to babysit us, a young teen named Ada D'Elia who we really liked. Harry loved her. He had such a personality and he was so cute that he just charmed all the people he met.

One night the doorbell rang and I answered it. No one was there. Again it rang. I went to the door and saw Uncle Joe hiding in the bushes. He said "Shh . . ." and I was quiet. Again the bell rang and Mom was annoyed. When she answered the door, he jumped out and scared her half to death! She loved him, and it was obvious he loved his sister Judy.

Vacations

We would take family vacations to Syracuse, New York, where we would visit Mom's family. We loved to go. We were very close to our cousin Jo Jo. We always stayed at his house, just two doors away from Grandma's. We always had so much fun with JoJo/Joey. We would do flips on his bed and he said it was okay. Our mom and dad would have killed us if we tried to do that at home. A few times Joey would hide in our car on our way back to the Island, hoping he wouldn't be found until it was too late to turn back, but Dad wasn't very happy about it, and he always seemed to find Joey before it was too late.

We also would visit my father's family in New Jersey to see our Uncle John, Dad's brother. He had two daughters, Penny and Marsha, who I thought were my cousins. It appeared to us that the girls lived with Uncle John because he always brought them to our house, and they were there when we would visit Uncle John. We enjoyed our time together and looked forward to our visits which were more frequent than our visits upstate. Eventually Dad told Toni and me that they were our half sisters and that our brother John was our half brother. The reason he told us was because Marsha and Penny were moving away with their mother and we wouldn't get to see them. Well, he decided to try to have at least Marsha come and live with us. Therefore he wanted us to know what was going on.

∗ ∗ ∗ ∗

It is the last day of second grade. Toni and I walk to school as always, and on the last day everyone receives their report card. I get mine and everyone is asking who my teacher is next year, and it says a second grade teacher . . . . At the bottom it says, "Report to second grade." I shouldn't be surprised, but I am embarrassed and upset. I'm so afraid because Dad will kill me now.

I was spanked very hard with my special red paddle when I couldn't tell time or spell a word. I can't imagine the spanking or beating that I'll receive for this failure of the whole grade; I am crying to the point of sobbing.

I meet up with Toni for the long walk home and she is devastated!!!! She doesn't understand. She keeps reading her report card and can't wrap her brain around the part where it says second grade, like mine. That **must** be a mistake because she is supposed to go into third grade!! She has done well and worked really hard. Why would she have to repeat?? (*In reality, Toni did not fail. The teacher said it would not hurt her to repeat the grade, and it would be better for us psychologically to hold us both back. Our parents decided as well that she should be kept back.*)

We cry all the way home and I feel so afraid, knowing that when Dad finds out it's going to be unbearable.

We arrive at the house and we are crying, and Mom couldn't care less. She says, "Whatever you do, don't tell your father. Marsha's dead. She was burned to death putting out the trash!" *Oh my God!! I love Marsha! Dad said she might come and live with us someday. (I could not imagine what Penny must have suffered through this tragedy.)*

Dad comes home and we get packed to go to New Jersey so Toni, Harry, and I can stay with our older cousins while Dad, Mom, and Uncle John and his wife Aunt Kay go to Indiana for the funeral.

The Four Seasons were popular then, and my cousin had their album and played it many times. The song "Rag Doll" was also played on the radio. So, that song always reminds me of Marsha. While we stayed in New Jersey I would be playing and I would be okay, and then it would occur to me that I failed my grade and Dad didn't know. I would then **experience** the fear and my heart would start to race, and I would be unable to think as my mind entered panic mode. I don't know how I calmed myself; I was very upset over Marsha and overwhelmed with fear of my certain demise.

Dad and Mom returned and Dad never mentioned our failure. I think that the loss of his daughter was more than he could handle. She was just 10 years old. Our repeating second grade was not that big of a deal in light of this tragedy.

∗ ∗ ∗ ∗

Dad and Mom got into a violent argument and my father was physically abusing my mom. He actually broke her ribs. Mom told us that he hit her because she overcharged at the store. She had run up a bill in the thousands. So Mom had to get a job to pay off this debt. Consequently, Mom was working nights for a while. I thank God that it was short lived because of what happened when she was not home. I must mention this, although I will not go into great detail, because these episodes had a profound impact on my psychological well being.

One evening Toni I were in bed. We had twin beds next to each other. Dad came into my bed and he had Toni join us; it was very strange because he had no clothes on. He began telling us that he was our father and we belonged to him. He said we had to learn about the birds and the bees. We were seven years old.

After that initial encounter, I cannot remember how many times Daddy would call us out to change the channel for him. Sometimes he would call Toni and he would say, "Go get Mary to come out." Many times when we would get ready for bed Dad would say to me, "After Toni is asleep, come out here." I knew what would happen, but I obeyed. I knew when he would plan the time for him and me, because the couch in the front room was pulled out and was now a bed. I was so desperate to receive love that I thought, *Well, maybe this is what makes me Daddy's special girl.* So, a part of my past misery was being sexually abused by my biological father. I know that it was not my fault, but for many years I blamed myself for the abuse. It was NOT LOVE; it was selfish on his part. This is never the child's fault. It is the adult who is responsible.

Dad also had a female over one night, and my mom figured out that her friend had been over. Mom was asking us what we heard. They had a big fight, and my father had a gun and he shot the mirror in their bedroom. It was just a BB gun; nonetheless it was extremely abusive to my mom because she loved her new furniture and he damaged it. He also broke her ribs one time when they were in a fight. He also broke my brother John's arm when he was little, because John was jumping on the bed. Dad was messed up and violent at times.

School Medical Exams

During the school year we had to get checkups. The school nurse would weigh us and check our height, hearing, and vision. This year the school nurse sent home a note saying that I needed to get my eyes checked. I understood that I might need glasses. Now, when I was in kindergarten I had an eye operation at age five for a lazy eye. I recall my mom being very concerned about me needing glasses, but the doctor said I didn't need them then. I thank God that my parents had the means to take care of me.

Now in second grade for the second time, it was determined that I might need glasses. Mom never took me to the doctor, though. She said, "They won't be twins if she gets glasses." My mom chose to ignore the note and I didn't go to the eye doctor as the note clearly recommended.

The next year I was in third grade and again the test was done. The school nurse was surprised that I didn't have glasses, knowing that last year I needed them. Again my mom ignored the request to have my eyes examined. I think she needed her head examined at this point. I was becoming more aware that something was wrong with her and my dad.

I continued to feel disconnected in school.

* * * *

Mom got really sick. She had cancer, she was hospitalized, and she was gone for three months. Some of our aunts and uncles came to visit her, as it was very serious. During this time I felt free. Mr. and Mrs. Doyle were taking care of Toni, Harry, and me.

I was so happy every day we came home and went to Mr.

and Mrs. Doyle's home. Mom was in the hospital for a LONG time. I didn't know that she was dying.

The days at the Doyles' were enjoyable; I wished that I could live there forever. *Maybe if Mom never comes home we could live with them.* Despite the fact that I was stupid, Mrs. Doyle was real nice and I wished she were my mom. I was playing upstairs the day my mom came home. Mrs. Doyle called to me, "Mary, your mom is home." I didn't want to leave; I continued to play. She called again but still I played. I was disobeying because I wished she had **never** come home! *Why did she have to come home?* I didn't want this time to end. I was attempting to drag it out. I knew what was going to happen and there would be no escape. Soon I would re-enter the war zone. *I am Mom's #1 enemy and no matter what I do I will always and forever be bad.* Mrs. Doyle came upstairs and spoke with me with that kind voice and told me that I had to go home. She was saying how much my mom missed me and how happy she would be to see me. I knew that Mrs. Doyle didn't know the secret. She had no idea what went on in the house next door. My mom couldn't care less if I came home; she had wished I was never born. She didn't want to see me, and I KNEW IT! I went home reluctantly, and Mom was livid! "I've been gone and you don't want to see me!!!" She hadn't changed since her near death experience. I wasn't surprised.

She was about 37 years old when she was diagnosed with cancer. She had 9 operations, and the doctors told my dad that she had 18 months to live.

Third Grade

In third grade, Toni's love for music was evident and she was thinking about what instrument she wanted to play. She decided to play clarinet. Toni didn't get to go into the band, because we moved.

I was moved up to the third grade reading group and had

a book just like Toni's. I continued to struggle, because I was actually doing both groups: the second grade book and the third grade book.

Although we were in different classes, for gym class we came together. We had to do calisthenics. One day Toni led the class and she was hilarious. Every girl was laughing so hard. Toni wouldn't do the exercises; she just started saying "GOOD JOB!" She began to lead the exercises and she did it in a humorous way, motivating the rest of the class.

The next week one of the other students led the group. We were sitting Indian style on the floor, legs crossed. All of us girls began to bang our hands on the gym floor, chanting over and over, "WE WANT TONI! WE WANT TONI! WE WANT TONI!!" The teacher let her do it but said that she had to exercise with the class. Toni was still an inhibited little girl inside, but when she led the class in calisthenics she was outgoing, funny, and amazing.

I prayed to St. Jude (the saint of hopeless cases) to help me to pass third grade and I DID!!! It was a shock because I always felt lost in class.

Fourth Grade

I didn't have any friends, but Toni made a friend and went to her house without me, which was new for us. Toni and I did everything together, so it was very different for Toni to have a friend who I didn't really know.

Mom was slowly recuperating from her near death episode. Dad's job was being moved to California, but we moved to Syracuse. Although I didn't want to move, there was a part of me that thought I might be able to start over and make new friends.

PART II
The Move Upstate - The Misery

I·t was April 1967; Toni and I were 10 years old and in fourth grade when 20th Century Fox moved out of New York City. My dad had a job waiting for him in California, but Mom was still sick and the doctors told my dad that she had 18 months to live. So Dad decided to move upstate to Syracuse to be near Mom's family.

He had a plan, because he knew that if and when she died there was no way that he was going to raise the three of us. So we moved upstate; I had always said Syracuse was a nice place to visit but I would never want to live there. Dad's plan was that when Mom died he could leave the three of us with her family and he would go to California. I know this because he told me when he was 60 years old and very sick that he had no intention of staying with us after Mom died. However, Mom did not die as expected. She lived until 1990.

Syracuse was very different from Plainview, Long Island. The most obvious difference was that in Long Island we had lived in a new home in a fairly new neighborhood. Grandma's home, where we now lived, was an older colonial. The sidewalk was also unique: one section had about 8-10 cool rectangular blocks of stone that were set in the cement.

We often entered Grandma's house through the side door. We would go up the four steps, knock, and then just enter; this seemed very strange to me. I was taught that one was to wait until the door was answered. I soon learned that this rule applies to others, outside of the family. This was **our** grandmother's house; therefore we were family.

This was a four-bedroom colonial, and the stairs had a light blue tile on them with a marble design. I actually liked this house, and I had a lot of good memories of it. Every time I had been there in the past it was to visit; now we were living there.

Next door to Grandma's was the D'Elia family; the home beyond that was obviously unkempt. I had never seen the woman who lived there, but she was referred to as the cat lady. The next home was Uncle Joe and Aunt Bev's. Their son was Joey, who we referred to as Jo Jo, and later on they had another boy named Michael. As I said earlier, they used to come and visit us on Long Island. When they did, they would bring as a babysitter Ada D'Elia. I now realized that Ada lived with her family right next door to Grandma's house. (Harry had a little crush on Ada, so he loved when she was there; he was only six years old. Years later Harry married her baby sister Wanda.)

Grandma's house was like Grand Central Station. I quickly adjusted to the constant visitors, who were all family. My mom had six brothers and two sisters, which resulted in a lot of cousins: 27 first cousins to be exact. So there was always someone stopping by to see my grandmother.

My grandmother was still working at Bristol Labs in 1967. My grandfather had passed away when I was seven or eight years old. I remember visiting when he died. My mom was hysterical, and so were her brothers and sisters; they all took it very hard.

They called him Pa. I remember him; he spoke mainly Italian and broken English. On one of our visits to Syracuse when we were young, maybe six years old, we went to Utica for the Utica Feast. This was a big event! The feast was a celebration of the saints; I'm not sure which ones but it was a very busy place. We went out to eat at a restaurant and everyone knew my grandfather. They knew that we were Prince girls and belonged to that family.

We moved to Grandma's house at 336 Elm Street. Toni and I were finishing up fourth grade at Cleveland School, which was also very different from Fern Place. Cleveland was on Winton Street and was an extremely old structure. If we had to use the rest room the proper request was "May I go to the basement?" I thought this an odd request until I realized that the rest rooms were in the basement of the school.

Toni and I went to Cleveland School for the rest of fourth grade. During this time we were living at Grandma's, and we were spending time with Joey and his buddies. We would play tom tom tackle and football. I was having a great time with my cousin Joey and his friends; I never played outside like this back home.

One day they were trying to get burdock in our hair; being a city girl I had never seen burdock. I knew, though, that it would be hard to get out of my hair, so I ran as they chased Toni and me. The wind was blowing very hard this day; I was having a great time until a piece of the burdock got into my eye!!!!

I suffered for three days before my grandmother told my mom to get me to the ER; everyone knew that I was in pain. Every day after school I would go to sleep for fear that the stabbing pain would return. When we got to the ER the doctor was really nice to me. He felt so bad, and when he removed the three pieces from my eye I thought he was going to call Child Protective Services, because he yelled at my mom, "ONE MORE DAY!!!! ONE MORE DAY!!!!" **He was pissed.** "She would have been blind in that eye." He seemed to care about me and think that I was worth something, and he knew that Mom was mistreating me in some way. Now, I did mention that at age five I had eye surgery in Long Island to get my eyes straight. I had weak eye muscles, and I am very grateful that my parents fixed my eyes. I'm very thankful for that surgery. So, when I got the burdock in my eye I was afraid to go to the doctor, but I **did** tell my mom, dad, and aunts that I had something in my eye.

* * * *

Years later, my husband said, "It seems as if your mom was overreactive to any illness you or your siblings had, and she rushed you to the ER when waiting to see the doctor would have been acceptable." He figured out that after the eye injury and the way the doctor reacted, it's possible that my mom said, "I'll show you. I'll bring the kids to the ER and no one will accuse me of neglect!" Also, being made to eat all of our food at the table could have been a reaction to being accused of not feeding John, because John was going around the neighborhood saying that he had no food. Consequently, she made us eat all of our food.

＊ ＊ ＊ ＊

For the first time Toni and I had an opportunity to witness what a healthy relationship looked like. We were living at Grandma's and there were just too many of us living there. With Mom, Dad, Toni, Harry, me, Uncle Sandy, Uncle Sam and Grandma, it was very crowded. Therefore, Toni and I moved up the street to stay with Aunt Helen and Uncle Frank and their two children, Tammy and Frankie. I loved it there. Aunt Helen and Uncle Frank were so good to Toni and me. I remember them talking to each other, and one time they were a bit upset; Uncle Frank said something and Aunt Helen said, "Not in front of the kids; we'll talk later." Toni asked Aunt Helen why she didn't want to talk to Uncle Frank then. Aunt Helen explained that later they could talk when they had thought about it and weren't angry. That would be a more productive conversation. I had never heard anything like that before, but it made sense.

One day it was really hot, and while Toni and I were getting ready for bed Aunt Helen said, "It will get cold tonight, so you'll need a blanket." She showed us where she kept them. I thought, *It's blazing hot out, I'm sure I won't need a blanket*, so when she showed me where they were I didn't pay attention. That night Toni and I woke up **so cold!!!** I tried to look in the closet, and Toni tried too, but we couldn't find the blanket. I thought to myself, *Why didn't you listen to her this afternoon?!* Toni and I paid the consequence during that sleepless night.

The next day I asked Aunt Helen where she kept the extra blankets; I told her how cold we had been. Aunt Helen asked, "Why didn't you wake me???" I said, "I didn't want you to get mad at me." She said, "Honey, I wouldn't get angry at you. All you had to do was knock on the door and I would have gotten the blanket for you." She really felt bad that we were cold. I could tell that **she loved Toni and me, and she didn't want me to be afraid of her or Uncle Frank.**

Meanwhile, Mom and Dad were not getting along . . . . There's a shock! Things were bad; Mom kept saying, "I'm giving him his walking papers!" She said it over and over again. Toni said she was nervous because she didn't know what Mom meant by walking papers, but she thought that it meant she was going to get a divorce. I had heard of divorce, and the thought of my parents getting one didn't upset me because they didn't get along, and then maybe we wouldn't have to listen to all of the fighting.

Mom was a go-getter. She had a lot of spunk. She got an apartment on Beech Street and Dad didn't move in with us. Mom's brothers were very protective of her. She had her brother Sam move in with us. She said that he was moving in to protect her from Dad and to help with the bills.

The best part about moving back with Mom was that we were with Harry again. We missed him very much.

Wanting to be accepted, I asked Mom if we could go to St. Vincent's and she said yes. I thought, *Great! I'll be in the same grade as one of Joey's friends.* He liked Toni and me; after all, we hung out all summer and he wanted us to go to his school.

Toni and I had strong Long Island accents. As a result, everyone wanted to hear our accent. Say this; say that. It was nonstop!!! Joey's friends liked to hear our accents as well. I didn't realize that I was being a phony at the time, but Toni and I practiced talking like Syracusans, and we did a pretty good job with it. Anytime I was really upset, though, the New York came out.

My mom would yell, "You lost your accent!" She was very angry about it. I just wanted to fit in and be accepted; I wanted friends. If that meant putting on a false, fake accent, then I had to do it.

We entered St. Vincent's and it was a big mistake. First, Mom could not afford the school. We ended up with used uniforms. The problem was that they were too big and needed to be hemmed. Mom didn't sew and Dad was not around, so we hemmed the navy blue jumpers ourselves. We were 11 years old, we didn't have a sewing machine, and we weren't taught how to sew properly. I didn't know that the excess fabric should be cut off. Therefore the jumpers didn't look as nice as the other girls'. The special Peter Pan collared shirt was expensive, so Mom had us just wear white oxford shirts under our jumpers, unlike the suggested uniform. All the girls would wear navy blue knee-high socks with the uniform. I thought that they looked really nice, so Toni and I also bought knee-high socks. The problem was that our legs were extremely thin, and the knee-highs were constantly falling down.

I didn't notice the difference on the first day, but as time went on I noticed how different Toni and I looked. I remember thinking, *Why do they look so nice?*

One day the nun took one of the girls to the front of the room and said, "This is how a uniform should look. Perfect! Now, how does your mother get this to look so nice?" The little girl said, "I don't know. She sends it out to the dry cleaners."

I thought, *Oh, I'll ask Mom if we can send the jumpers to the cleaners, and then we'll look like the other girls, and maybe we can get the right shirts.* Mom said no; we couldn't afford it.

Academics

The work was really hard and the nun was abusive!!! Eventually she was removed from her position, because one of the students documented every abusive act. She pulled Toni's and my hair when she walked by our desks, saying that she didn't approve of hair hanging down. Toni and I understood that statement all too well. We were told since age four that our hair was ugly.

St. Vincent's was really hard and we didn't fit in. My cousin Joey's friend wanted us to hang with the cool kids, but I picked the wrong friend and he separated himself from Toni and me. There were probably other reasons, one being academic— Toni and I were having an awful time. First of all, we both needed glasses to see the board. Not being able to see clearly affected our academic performance. Another reason Joey's friend may have pulled away was the fact that we were wearing used uniforms and looked awful! They were pilling, and I didn't have the cognitive ability at 11 years old to realize that the jumpers needed to be dry-cleaned, and because they were never dry-cleaned they were ruined. I didn't realize that Toni and I were the "needy kids." I just felt the pain of rejection. There was no place of refuge; home was worse than ever. I don't know who paid our tuition. Perhaps we were just charity cases.

We were living on Beech Street. My mother's brother was living with us; Dad was not living there but he would often come over to the apartment. Dad would be drunk and Mom would call the police because she wanted him out. I remember running down the stairs in fear of my dad. I know that my mom would call her brothers Joe and John, and they would come to her rescue. (Uncle Sam was out of town at times for work.) The fact was that Uncle Joe would fight with my father. Uncle Joe had boxed in Golden Gloves tournaments and won; therefore, it was obvious that my dad was messing with the wrong family.

While in Long Island I felt lost and alone, an outsider who could not enter into the secret club of understanding. Well, things went from bad to worse. Home was chaos and we were being picked on at school. Now not only was my home life constant torture, school also became a living hell. I don't recall the first time I heard the buzzing sound. I had no idea at first that the noise was directed at my twin and me. I'm not certain why, but we were being called "the bees." Someone said, "It's because you sleep in class and bees sleep a lot." Well, with the chaos at home, who could sleep there?

I felt betrayed when one of Joey's friends was buzzing at us. I have no doubt that he was torn; wanting to be a part of his group he didn't have a choice, and I don't blame him. I wanted to go to that school because I liked him and I thought that he liked Toni and me. He wanted us to go to his school. Actually, he was the first boy that I had a crush on. I ask myself why we weren't accepted. Was it because one of the girls was trying to choose our friends, or was it the uniforms, or our oily hair? I guess the list could go on and on. The name-calling became unbearable!!!

This was extremely hurtful. I became an emotional ball of anger, so hard that no one knew me except Toni, Harry, and my closest friend Tina Bufano. Tina saw the hard Mary, but there was something about me that she liked. Toni and I were also very close to our younger cousin Toni Collins. She looked up to us and always wanted to stay overnight at our house. Her mom was my mom's sister. We loved having her over.

∗ ∗ ∗ ∗

The teasing increased and it was overwhelming. I became angry and depressed. I had been so hurt. I wanted to tell my mom, but she couldn't understand and her response was, "I always had a lot of boyfriends when I was your age. I don't know what's wrong with you two." It was around this time when we were 11 years old that she began to make negative comments about our bodies. She said on numerous occasions that we looked like we came from a concentration camp! I sank into a depressed state; I was feeling less and less of self. I began to hate me.

Living on Beech Street

The one thing that I missed terribly while living with Aunt Helen and Uncle Frank was my brother Harry. I wondered if he was safe and if he was happy. When we moved to the apartment, though, I was able to see him every day. Toni and I learned fast that Mom was not a morning person. So the goal each morning before school was to get out of the house without waking her. Toni and I had an alarm clock, and we would get up and then wake up Harry. It was during this time that the bathroom became the gathering place for the three of us. We would brush our teeth and help Harry get ready for school. Getting breakfast we had to be very quiet, because Mom's bedroom was off the kitchen.

She was very angry with me during this time, and she was frustrated because I couldn't do the schoolwork. Mom would talk about picking beans on the farm and not beginning school until November. She said, "I didn't get to go to school until November and I still had A's. I never failed a grade and I didn't even begin in September like the other kids. I was smart! I don't know what is wrong with you. I was NEVER STUPID LIKE YOU TWO!!!"

During fifth grade we moved from Beech Street to 1200 Hawley Ave. We lived in the bottom floor flat, and my mom was very happy about the new apartment. We had been evicted from Beech Street, I think because Mom called the police one too many times on Dad. Although they were separated, it was very confusing because he was always trying to get back into our lives. Mom was talking about getting a divorce at this time, and her paranoia became all consuming.

I watched as she looked out the window. "Mary, see that car over there? He was here an hour ago. . . . He's an investigator."

It was during this time that I first noticed that Mom was paranoid. Mom thought that there were people watching her. She was always counting and re-counting her cash. She was disabled due to her cancer, but was helping her brother Joe at the bar. Of course, he gave her a little extra money; she was just making pizzas, so it wasn't hard work but the hours were long. Perhaps she thought that she was wrong to sell the pizzas and the paranoid thinking kicked in; I am not too sure, but she began to put the money in her sock. This was when the "good twin," Toni, had to help Mom count the money and listen to what she had to say.

Mom would make Toni go into our bathroom with her and she wouldn't let her leave. She **had** to stay in there to help count the money.

Mom would put her money in her socks and she would say, "I'm clean and the money doesn't smell."

I knew that she was strange, but at 11 years old I had no understanding of mental illness.

She seemed to think that the house was bugged and the phone tapped. She would call my father "the big guy" because he was not to be living with us, but she took him back after he OD'ed on sleeping pills. She said he took three bottles!!! Then she said, he should have taken **four** bottles!! I felt bad that he tried to kill himself; and Mom wished that he had succeeded.

My dad was put into Marcy State Hospital for the DTs (Delirium Tremens). Later, he was transferred to the Veterans Hospital in Syracuse. Mom would drive us to the VA and we would wait in the car while she visited.

Mom made sure that she pointed out the bars on the windows. She said, "That's where your father is because he's crazy! And to think he tried to blame me when he was at Marcy!!!"

Around this time it was just the three of us: Toni, Harry, and me. Toni and I cooked and cared for Harry. While Mom was hustling her pizzas, Harry was out playing with his friends. He must have missed Mom, but at least it was quiet when she wasn't home. Harry was well liked and had a lot of friends. For years he was close to Mark Fregin, and I didn't realize the positive impact Mark's mom had in my brother Harry's life. She was like a mother to him, and the three of us desperately needed for that void to be filled.

Meanwhile, Dad was in the hospital.

Also during this time we had that same male relative still living with us, and he had one of the same problems as my dad. It happened when Toni was down in the basement doing the laundry. Unfortunately, this abuse occurred a few more times. Toni became afraid to go to the basement out of fear that this relative would follow her. Finally, she said something to our mom about what was going on. She didn't really tell her everything, but did say that this relative put his hand on her and she felt uncomfortable. We were glad when Mom confronted him and then kicked him out of the house.

I felt bad for Toni because every time she saw this individual afterwards, he gave her dirty looks like she had done something wrong and not him.

* * * *

Toni and I failed fifth grade. The work at the private school was advanced, and we did not have our glasses and we really needed them at this point. We did make one really good friend, though: Tina Bufano.

We had to go to summer school for math. Although we failed the grade we were behind in math and had to take the class just to re-enter fifth grade. The problem was that the private school did not offer the summer school class; therefore we had to go to a school that wasn't near our home. Mom would have to drive us. I never liked to get up in the morning. The alarm would go off and Toni would get up first and then wake me after she was done with the bathroom.

Mom woke up. I didn't know what happened, but she wanted me out of that bed NOW!!!! She pulled my hair and it hurt. I found myself trapped against the wall. I didn't know what was happening at first; I didn't know how this was supposed to work. I heard her saying, "IF YOU TWO WEREN'T SO STUPID, I wouldn't have to get up and take you to school. I NEVER WAS STUPID LIKE YOU! I HATE YOU!" Her fists would fly; my head hurt and I tried not to let her hit me. I put my arms up to protect my head.

My brother Harry would be in the hallway crying, **pleading,** "MOMMY, STOP." Harry was about eight years old. He was standing there helpless and scared. He wanted to help rescue me, and he was desperate to help, but he was just a little boy. There was no way he could have pulled her off of me. I envision a mad dog attacking and Harry watching helplessly. Toni would talk to Mom, trying to reason with her, to somehow make her see that she needed to stop. The rampage continued: "I WAS UP WITH YOUS TWO FOR **A YEAR!!!!!**" She pulled my hair and beat it into me that I was stupid and ugly. She said, "YOU LOOK LIKE YOU COME FROM A CONCENTRATION CAMP!!! I never was stupid like yous." Eventually I began to block her punches. I never remember any bruises.

Maybe if this were a onetime incident it would be okay, but it went on every morning. By the time Toni and I went to class, we had NO clue as to what we were learning. I sank into depression. I was alone and unwanted, and mostly UNLOVED. Although I knew that Toni and Harry loved me, the darkness of the depression overtook me. I don't know why. I began to hit myself while looking in the mirror; I even pulled my Indian straight hair. The self-inflicted violence began; the self-loathing was overwhelming. I asked God, "Why did you make me so ugly?" While in summer school I was again in that place of disconnect. I was tired and fell asleep in class, never knowing what was taught. It was no use; I couldn't do the work.

Toni said that she also was tired. It was the last or close to the last day of summer school, and the teacher presented a fun math problem. Toni said she was kind of excited, because **today** was our birthday and when you were done with the problem the teacher would know your birthday—**if** you did it correctly. When Toni did it wrong, she was distressed. Making the mistake solidified her belief that she must be stupid. I felt sad because it was our birthday, and it would have been nice to have something good come out of the day. I didn't even **attempt** to do the problem, but I did think that **Toni** would be able to accomplish the task. It turned out that Toni made a mistake with her computations and the teacher was not able to disclose the fact that it was our birthday that very day. I remember how Toni became unglued, and it was as if she were traumatized. **I couldn't console her;** she was devastated.

The turning point came when somewhere in the midst of the darkness I decided that all we learn in school is unnecessary; who needs it??? Hell, I'm going to get married and have a family. Therefore, I DO NOT NEED math!! It's all bullshit. I decided that I didn't give a shit about school, or Mom. I just prayed to God with Toni every night that we would have HAPPY, healthy marriages. That is all I wanted. I wanted to be loved. I had decided that I must be married before I turned 20.

* * * *

Something changed in me that summer: I was ready for a fight. Any kindness was extinguished and I was not going to take it anymore. I had emerged from the darkness of despair and depression, and I no longer was my own **main** target. The fighter was born.

We repeated fifth grade and it was then that we got our eyeglasses; I was amazed that the chalk on the board makes a straight line!!! I thought that the chalk made a thick, fuzzy line like when you lay the chalk on its side. It was no surprise that I hated geography; I could never distinguish between the states, or the countries for that matter. I never saw the lines on the maps.

Home life was worse than before. I wished I could have stayed with Aunt Helen and Uncle Frank. Aunt Kathy was also nice, and she would come over to visit and would listen to Toni and me as if we were important. That was awesome.

Mom also continued to point out that our bodies were unacceptable. She said, "You are so skinny that you both look like you come from a concentration camp!!" *Oh, like I NEVER HEARD THAT BEFORE. IT WAS GREAT THAT SHE RE-PEATED HERSELF OVER AND OVER, JUST IN CASE I DIDN'T HEAR HER THE HUNDRED TIMES SHE SAID IT IN THE PAST YEAR!* I didn't know what she meant, but I knew that it was bad. I became more self-conscious and aware that we were really ugly. It was as though I was ashamed to be seen. *Maybe I should go into the house and come out with a bag over my face, because no one wants to look at us.*

Toni and I **refused** to wear shorts or short-sleeve shirts. Every day, no matter how hot and humid it got, we wore long-sleeve shirts and jeans. There was no way that Toni or I would let anyone see our arms and legs. I hated my legs, and some-times Mom would hear me say that I hated my legs and she would say, "Be glad that you can walk!"

Failing fifth grade solidified the fact that I was stupid. I had made a mess of everything. Toni and I were the mock-outs of the class. Some classmates may have known that we were on welfare and received food stamps. I felt so different from the other kids; I was painfully aware of my low IQ and inferior body shape.

Tina maintained our friendship although we were mock-outs. I didn't understand why she hung with us despite the fact that she was now in sixth grade and we stayed in fifth.

The first day of fifth grade the teacher left the room, and I stood up and told the class, **"You will not be calling us the bees!!! I better not hear any buzzing sounds ever!"** As I stated, the fighter was born and ready to hurt those before they hurt me. Whatever I said that day it stuck, and the class never called us bees. In fact, sometimes they would tease one of the boys for getting a buzz cut. Prior to buzzing, they would let me know that they were going to tease one of the guys about the haircut. It was not directed at Toni or me.

I saw all authority as the enemy. My mom and dad were off and on; one day he was there and the next he was not. I didn't know if they were together or what they were doing, and it was very confusing. The police were called often because Mom and Dad were fighting. He would get so drunk, and then the violence would begin. My mom had an order of protection against my dad, but every time the police came to the house they would take him for a WALK!!! I used to think, *What the hell!! How is taking him for a walk going to fix this problem?* I never understood that, but he did cool off and leave all of us alone . . . until the next time.

During this time there was a popular girl who began to ask me, "Why are you so skinny?" This girl was tall compared to my 4 ft. 11 stature. Due to my history of abuse, I became very angry. I was used to my mom saying negative things to Toni and me, **but who the hell did she think she was?!** I told her to watch her back on the last day of school. She didn't seem to understand what I was saying. I had learned from my cousin Joey that if you can wait until the last day of school to kick someone's ass, you won't reap the consequence because what are they going to do to you? Suspend you? Duh . . . .

On the last day of school I went after her. I knew a little boxing because my cousin Joey taught us. Also, there was a girl

(Mary Ann) who worked with me on my boxing for about a week straight. So on the last day of school I went after her and I was hitting her. I got her in a headlock, and her big brother tapped me on the back and said, "It's over, enough." I had to stop. This guy was about 5 ft. 7 but seemed like 6 ft. I didn't mind that the fight ended; I sensed an empowering that day. I had the fight in me, so others knew I was not making idle threats.

Although this one girl and I had a problem, most of the new group of students were nicer to us than the former class. In fifth grade Toni sat behind me, next to a kid named Rob. They got along really well. I still got nervous when I was called on to read out loud.

Summer 1969, Aunt Kathy

Despite the fact that I was very angry and fighting, at times the shame and self-loathing were unbearable at times. Aunt Kathy lived with Grandma and her husband, my mom's brother Uncle Santo. We called him Uncle Sandy. My mom got along with her, and Aunt Kathy was often at our house. Ever since we moved up here she took an interest in Toni and me.

She would visit on Hawley Ave. and sit at the kitchen table and talk with us. I loved her, and I thought it was great that someone cared about what was important to Toni and me. My mom would get aggravated and would yell at us to leave Aunt Kathy alone! But she would say, "Judy, they're not bothering me."

Mom would scream about our long hair and Aunt Kathy would say, "Of course they want it long; it's the style."

Mom argued, "They look the same going to bed as when they get up!"

Aunt Kathy would just calm her down. She never put my mom down; she would just love and support us. She was and is amazing.

During the very dark times after we failed fifth grade, Aunt Kathy reached out to us. She understood Toni and me; as a result we spent a lot of time together. Aunt Kathy noticed that Toni and I were wearing long pants and long-sleeve shirts when it was 90 degrees and humid. One day she said, "It's so hot out today. Put on your shorts and short-sleeve shirts."

Toni and I told her we didn't want anyone to see our skinny arms.

Aunt Kathy said, "People will think you're shooting up dope, doing drugs, and that you're trying to hide track marks." She said that there was nothing wrong with our arms or legs.

Around that time Twiggy won the Miss America Beauty Pageant. Toni and I were walking to Shop City on Teall Ave. and some guys yelled out the window to us, "HEY TWIGGY!!" We were deeply hurt because we heard people saying that Twiggy was too thin. When we told Aunt Kathy about it, she turned the whole thing around and said, "That's a compliment!!!" Although I didn't believe her, I so appreciated that she thought Toni and I were okay.

Eventually, Toni and I slowly began to wear short-sleeve shirts, but we REFUSED to wear shorts!

Another problem was that Toni and I needed to wear bras.

Again, Aunt Kathy had to help my mom guide us. She told Mom it was way overdue, so Mom finally took us to buy bras. By the time we each got one, we were long past the training bra stage and felt very embarrassed. When I think of that, I wonder what people must have thought: PUT ON A BRA! Toni and I just didn't know.

We needed to shave and Mom said, "No! If you shave the hair will come in coarse. Wait." We did wait, until Aunt Kathy took Toni and me into the bathroom and showed us how to do it. She was truly a godsend!!

It was comforting to have Aunt Kathy as a positive adult in our lives. She seemed to think that we were okay, normal in some way. I honestly do not know what would have happened to me without her.

Sixth Grade, 1969-1970

Toni and I passed fifth grade and went to sixth. Finally. What a **miracle!**

We hung out with the boys. The girls were very cliquey; they looked down on us and didn't accept us in their exclusive group. Back home Dad had returned. I was now 12 going on 13. Toni and I were very thin but were developing. Being as thin as we were—almost 5 feet and only 94 pounds—our breasts appeared large. One adult male we knew would tease us and say, "You going to play basketball?" He was referring to the bouncing of our chests. We became uncomfortable with our breasts.

Back home, Dad was regressing to old behaviors. He would have me sit next to him on the couch, and he began to feel my breasts. I wanted to scream. I jumped the first time he did this, and he acted like this was something he had to do. I told Mom and she became very angry with me. I was so confused. The reality is that his behaviors progressed, and he began to come into my room at night. Toni slept on the top bunk, I on the bottom. Toni knew what he was doing to me, but she was too afraid to help. When Mom would attack me, she stood up for me and was able to talk to Mom and have her stop the beatings. However, she was unable to stop Dad from molesting me. She lay paralyzed in her bed.

When I was seven, I didn't know what to do. Now, at age 12, I thought that because I hadn't told on him **when I was little,** maybe he figured that I liked it and I was at fault. I told my Mom that he came into our room, and she was pissed . . . **at me.** It was somehow my fault that he did this to me. We got a lock on the bedroom door so at night he couldn't get in. Eventually Mom did confront him about the abuse. He said, and I quote, "They are my girls and I can do whatever I want to. They are MINE." With that confession she kicked him out of the house again.

The whole family knew the secret. I felt ashamed, embarrassed that everyone knew. I became suspicious of everyone and I was overprotective of Harry. He had no idea that I was afraid that Mom might be touching him. *(She never did.)*

We were involved in the St. Peter's bowling league, and when Toni and I came home one Saturday, Mom was drunk and was dancing with Harry in the living room where she slept. I was so angry. I said, "What are you doing??" "WE'RE DANCING," she yelled, as she spun Harry around. I did **not** like this at all. I asked him if she hurt him and he said no. She then began to say that it was my fault that she was alone. "I had to kick Dad out because of **you!**" (Harry later told us that he was upset that day because Mom was drunk and was rough with him, saying "Dance! Dance, you bastard!")

It was always my fault, no matter what happened. I was having a difficult time figuring out the part that I was responsible for. Toni and I went to a group for children of broken homes, and I related to some of those kids. They were troubled, and I knew that I was troubled as well. One area of confusion, though, was that I wasn't certain my parents were actually divorced like these other kids' parents. I wanted to fit in, but not knowing for sure if my parents were together or not made me feel like I didn't.

There was this cycle of in and out: one day Dad was gone and then he was back.

Mom continued to blame me for the fact that Dad was not living with us. I listened and I said, **"Do whatever you want!!"** She eventually did—she brought him back home. This cycle continued for years. Thank God the sexual abuse did not resume; I was glad that we had the lock on the door; I remember hearing him trying to open the door a few times, but the lock deterred him. I know that one time he was plastered and he took all his clothes off in the front room. We were told not to go out there: "Dad is in his birthday suit." The fights did break out in the night. We would be sound asleep and wake up to yelling and things breaking. Mom would be screaming, "I want you out of here!"

One night the fighting got intense and Dad was chasing Mom. She ran out to the back porch and he was all over her. He was hitting her and I think he was going to push her off the porch, which was pretty high. I grabbed hold of his pajamas at the shoulder and they ripped. I don't know why he stopped; perhaps it surprised him.

The next day he asked ME to sew the pajamas for him. I thought, *He has got to be kidding me. What the—? Man!* The fact is that he was my father, and he had the power to tell me what to do. There was no choice; I had to do what he told me. The sense of helplessness envelops me again.

∗ ∗ ∗ ∗

Some good memories with my dad were when I was on the bowling team at St. Vincent's. Toni would have her guitar lesson. Toni always had a love for music and she wanted lessons, so I asked Mom if she could have them. Dad would pick us up, and Dad, Harry, Toni, and I would go out for pizza. We were welcome in this restaurant and it became an ongoing treat. The waitress was awesome, and she would put a reserved sign on our favorite table; Dad would listen to us talk. It was weird but he was really nice. He would always drink and he was drunk by time we would leave, but for some reason these dinners were special and enjoyable. I think that the waitress viewed us as a happy family.

We all thought, *wouldn't it be nice if Mom joined us?* Let's just say that we were wrong. Mom came one time and it was so embarrassing. She was saying negative things about the waitress and was angry with Dad. When the bowling league ended, so did our nights out for dinner. I won a trophy for highest score by a woman bowler with a 155. That was not my highest game, but it was for our small league.

During two of our summers, Toni, Harry, and I were involved with St Peter's Church youth. In the summer we would go bowling on Tuesdays and Thursdays. We would also have group guitar lessons. Toni worked really hard and was in the highest group the second year we did it, and they gave her a guitar. Harry and I did very well at bowling. Harry got a trophy, and I was in a tournament and also got a trophy. I bowled a 191.

As I think of this time, I remember Dad bought me a watch and it looked just like his but smaller. Wide bands were in style and I was hoping to have a cool one. It turns out that I could remove the band and buy a new one, so I went to the drug store—Fays Drug Store in Shop City. I went in and couldn't decide if I wanted the blue or the black band. I chose the black one, but as I walked out of the store I changed my mind. I went back in and told the cashier, and she said just to go make the exchange. I did, and on my way out the security guard stopped me and accused me of stealing. I became irate. I was so angry! *I DID NOT TAKE ANYTHING!!!!!! HOW COULD HE ACCUSE ME? I'M INNOCENT!!!* It figures that I looked like a thief. Well, then I must have taken it. This was one of the first times I verbally lashed out at an authority figure.

Being angry all of the time was exhausting. My classmates feared me; they knew that I was older and tough. Toni and I did not have any female friends other than Tina, who was a grade ahead.

During this time I developed a sense of who I was, and I realized that I was a kid from a broken home and that I was ugly and different. I knew for certain that my intellect was below normal! I could not achieve. It was a miracle that I passed sixth grade.

* * * *

It was Halloween and I was next door with the neighbors. She asked if I would go get her son from a party. He was a year younger than I was. I kind of liked him and it was a nice evening. I liked being outside, so I was glad to help out. I asked her to tell my mom where I was. I thought that since she was an adult, all was cool. I got her son and I think his sister was with him, but we took our sweet time returning home.

I was blindsided as I entered through the back door. Mom says, "Dad wants you." I am 12 or 13; I sense the tension and I think, *What is going on? I was asked by an adult to get the kids.*

I enter the front room and I don't know what he is saying; all I remember is the fear that grips me. He has that red paddle—the thick one—in his hand. He says, "GET OVER HERE!" I walk over and I think, *He's not going to hit me, is he???* He grabs my arm and smacks my butt with the paddle really hard. I refuse to cry. He does it again and it BREAKS! God it hurts, but I still refuse to cry. I am thinking that the neighbor didn't tell Mom that I did her the favor, but they are in no mood to hear my explanation. Of course Dad is smashed. Mom yells at him for hitting me so hard. She says, "What are you doing?!!! You broke the paddle!"

"What do you want from me?!!!!"

"I asked you to correct her."

"I did, and now I didn't do it the way YOU wanted me to."

That was the last time I recall him beating me.

* * * *

We did not fit in with the girls in the class, but the guys all seemed to think we were okay. It was during the winter in sixth grade when one of the boys (I don't recall who) was fooling around and threw snow at me. The fight was on. Typically, when the guys threw a snowball the girls would scream and run. I of course retaliated and would fight back, and the guys were okay with that. It was at this time that I began to feel accepted by some of the class. I would sneak up on the guys and jump on their backs, and they would yell, "It's a Haupt!!"

They knew it was Toni or me. St. Vincent's became a safe place. The guys accepted Toni and me; I became close with Joe S. and Toni with Sam M.

School was **no longer** a living hell. We had friends; we went to the dances at school and the basketball games. Toni and I had tried out for cheerleading but did not make the team and gave up trying. One year there was a girls' basketball team, though, and Toni did very well. She would almost always make the layup, so the strategy was to put Toni at the basket and get the ball to her. Most of the kids had their parents there watching them at the home games. Of course that was not what happened for us.

Harry also made the basketball team, and though it was never spoken it was expected that we attend each other's games. Toni and I would go to Harry's and he would come to ours. One time he didn't show and I was so upset; I didn't realize at the time, but we had expected from each other what our parents could not give us: support and unconditional love.

Walking home from St. Vincent's, I was not far from my house and one of the boys in my class, Mike, started to say, "Hey, is that the big chief?" He was mocking my dad for his Native American heritage. Once again someone had something to say about someone else's ethnicity. My mom was always calling my father a drunken Indian bastard. He would call her a Guinea. The ethnic slams were common in our home, and I ingested the words and owned them as a part of who I was. My identity was developing and I continued to see myself as **less** than others—not just unattractive but stupid.

* * * *

Entering seventh grade was okay; I now had a reputation for being violent. I was hanging with Tina Bufano and Toni. I was also friends with Joe S. We were great friends and I felt close to him. I used to say that he was like a brother, and he never had a sister so he said that I was like a sister. One interesting fact is that his mother once dated one of my uncles when they were young; we would kid around and say that we could have been cousins if his mother had stayed with my uncle. Don was a new kid that year and he got along with Toni and me. He was a godsend, and I know that his positive influence was a key to Toni and me being accepted. Toni was hanging around the sixth graders and they loved her.

Finally the tide was turning for us. School was no longer a place of torment since I obtained the respect of others through violence. I continued to struggle academically, but at least our peers accepted us.

I was having an awful time with math, and it was at this point that I knew I could not do the work. I brought home the first report card and Dad was not happy. He said, "Why can't you do as well as Toni?!"

Again I was seen as lazy!!!!! I gave up totally, and I asked this one kid in class who was so smart if I could cheat off of his paper. This was the first time I cheated, but I thought that I didn't have a choice.

He was a good kid—clean cut and not one who would cheat. I don't know why he agreed to it, but because of his willingness to let me copy off of his paper my grade went from a 60 to a 78!! My grade improved by 18 points, and my father still wasn't happy because it wasn't as high as Toni's.

I had no idea why I could not grasp the work, but the reality is that I suffered through school. I was labeled **lazy and stupid.** I realized that whatever I achieved would never be good enough, so I gave up cheating because it didn't change anything.

During this time I was trying to be good. Toni got upset each time I caused trouble or got into a fight, and I didn't want to upset her, so I was **really trying to be good.**

The class is shaped like a squared U; my seat is dead center. The teacher leaves the room, and while she is out I am quiet and have made a decision to be good. The class is out of control: erasers are flying and kids are yelling, but as I said, I'm being good. The teacher comes into the room and says, "MISS HAUPT, your voice is the **ONLY** one I hear. MOVE YOUR DESK!"

I was stunned. I was totally, completely silent. She was a liar! I didn't understand where she wanted me to move my desk. *And why? I'M INNOCENT FOR ONCE!!!* **Man, I was so angry.** I moved my desk towards her, pushing it, and it was a good thing it didn't tip over because I was **enraged!!!** I was once again in trouble, and **I had done nothing wrong!!! How unfair!** Toni could not believe it. How could the teacher say such a thing? *My sister wasn't doing anything!* And who could even hear one voice over the chaos?

I was a very angry kid, and I was constantly on the defensive. It was exhausting to be angry all the time, but having that tough exterior gave me a sense of power and safety.

We graduated from 8th grade and I was upset that we had to wear dresses for the ceremony. Although we wore a uniform every day I was used to that. NOW to have to wear a dress! I was disgusted and I was angry; I didn't want anyone to see my legs! At school we wore knee socks, but with a dress we had to wear stockings! Wearing a dress with stockings was like being naked. Toni and I would be exposed; everyone would see **"the legs."** Mom had beaten it into us that our legs were embarrassingly skinny, and that she was totally disappointed by our legs and arms. After years of demeaning statements, she was puzzled that we said things like **"I hate my legs."** The thought of them being exposed was frightening. The fear immediately turned to anger. We went through the torment. I say torment, because I felt so ashamed of my legs that they seemed like some deformity that should be kept private.

Now Toni and I were behind two grades, graduating from 8th grade when we should have been completing 10th. Because we were on the small side, it wasn't obvious that we were behind. We were actually two of the shortest girls in the class. Despite that, our sense of self was destroyed.

I had begun to smoke cigarettes around this time.

In order to get into Bishop Grimes High School (BG) we had to take a placement test, and we did pretty badly. However, we were accepted and that was exciting for us.

The only reason we wanted to go to BG was so that we could be with Tina Bufano. After all, going to a new school is a big deal, so we thought if we went where we knew someone that might make it easier.

The uniforms at BG were nice, and Toni and I were getting new ones, NOT hand-me-downs! I knew that was going to make all the difference in the world; we would match and blend in. There were these blue blazers that were nice, I thought, because they looked like sport coats. I was so happy to have a new uniform. We entered BG and the first day I realized that we were **not to wear** the blazers, because NO ONE wore them; they were not cool. So we were to wear navy blue sweater vests!!! Of course we didn't have the right ones and ours looked different than the other girls'. I was trying so hard to fit in. But whatever we wore never seemed to be like the other girls'.

Summer of 1972: Moving Next Door to Grandma's

Mom was so proud of herself that she got out of the apartment and bought a home in her "stomping grounds." We moved to 334 Elm Street, right next door to Grandma's. She told us NEVER to sell this house—the "casa" as she would call it in Italian. One might think that this was the ideal set up, living next door to her mother with her brother Joe, Aunt Bev, and their two boys, Joey and Mike, living two doors away. Living next door to them were Uncle Sam along with Uncle Sandy, Aunt Kathy, and their two children, Santo and Antoinette. (Later they had a third, little Johnny.)

This made it convenient for rescue, so when my dad was drunk Mom would just call her brother Joe and he would come to her rescue. My dad would say, "Go ahead and call your brother! He kicked my ass before, he can do it again." I recall **one time** Mom was SCREAMING at the top of her lungs. She opened the windows and began to yell at the neighbors, calling them "motherf - - - - ." I was relieved that she wasn't directing that anger towards me. I'm not exaggerating at all, but that is what we had to put up with.

As I've said, I didn't trust her and I thought that she might be abusing my brother. She would go into the bathroom and think **nothing** of coming out in front of us with no top on, no bra!!!! Her behavior was bizarre. Harry said that she never abused him sexually, though. Thank God . . . . I didn't trust anyone!!

Her rage would always return to me. She would spend hours in the bathroom and would yell at me, kind of talking to herself because none of us could take listening to the constant putdowns. By this point in our lives, my mom would scream bloody murder at me: **"I HATE YOU."** I did at one point say to her, "I heard you the first time. **I get it!! You hate me and you wish I was never born!"** I didn't raise my voice, but I would repeat what she said. She would pretend to cry; it seemed like she was faking it. She would say, "I have no tears left."

* * * *

These tirades of anger towards me continued until she died. I remember my husband being fed up with her putting me down; he thought it was a shame that she never knew her own daughter. Toni spent many days listening to her yell about me. All she did was try to please Mom, but it never did work. Toni would always stick up for me. When she did, Mom said she wished she only had one daughter so she wouldn't have to share her. Mom was unable to manage her emotions. She had the ability to love; my mom was very close to one of our cousins, Toni Collins. She just loved her, and so did we. She also showed affection to some of our other cousins, and even had our cousin Michelle live with us for a while.

I was smoking often by that summer. Mom kept some cigarettes in the medicine cabinet, so I would help myself. I had been smoking as much as I could for about two years, but that was the summer that I began to buy my own cigarettes.

★ ★ ★ ★

At Bishop Grimes I met Linda Sorrendino and Meg Zaparo. They were friends, and Meg was dating my cousin Joey.

While at BG, Toni and I were put into the non-Regents classes, which to us felt like the "special class." The 9th grade math was algebra, but the special class broke the 9th grade math into two years so we could learn at a snail's pace. Now this was embarrassing and we were looked at as less than intelligent, and even stupid. (Again, that is how **we** perceived it.) I just thought, *Oh well . . . whatever.* **Toni, though, was disappointed, to say the least!!** She thought she could do the work!!! And she did. By December the teacher was trying to get her into Regents classes. Toni worked really hard, and I teased her and called her a bookworm. I guess she really liked algebra and was surprised it was so easy for her—fun too.

She never did get into the regular class, but in 9th grade Toni would be shown the problem and then go around the class and help everyone. She never did the work until the test, and then she would get 100.

October 1972

During that fall, Tina and I went on a hayride with the CYO (Catholic Youth Organization) at Blessed Sacrament. While on this hayride I met a boy named Pete. We hit it off and soon we began to date. He was on the Henninger basketball team. However, the relationship did not last and it ended on a bad note. During this time we hung out with my Aunt Kathy and helped her get her home painted on Aberdeen Terrace. We had a lot of good times together, but we were young and the relationship with Pete was unhealthy.

Though I shouldn't have stayed in an unhealthy relationship, I didn't know that it was unhealthy. I wanted to be loved so desperately that I thought he loved me.

I was very happy to be going to the Bishop Grimes dance on Oct 27, 1972 with my boyfriend. I couldn't believe that I had one. While at the dance, though, he said that he was breaking up with me.

I began to cry hysterically! I couldn't bear the thought of him leaving me. I was an unstable individual. I immediately called my Aunt Kathy and was crying on the phone. She said, "Don't let him see you cry."

I was so confused. Well, someone told him how upset I was and he saw me on the phone. He said, "Mary, I was only kidding. You know that."

I did not know that.

We left the dance and went across the street to the back parking lot of this business. He had some beer and we began to drink. I drank a lot. We never went back to the dance; we just got drunk and kissed.

When we returned to the school just as the dance was getting over, I went to open the door and I smashed my tooth on the door. I was trying to open it the wrong way.

I chipped my front left tooth that night and it didn't hurt. I knew that was due to the alcohol level in me; I didn't feel a thing.

We didn't last a month before we broke up.

* * * *

I began to hang with Linda and Meg, who were a lot of fun. Linda smoked cigarettes and so did I, so we of course would smoke in the girls' bathroom. One day Linda and I were in there having a cigarette. While Linda was exhaling the nun walked in and she was busted. I felt really bad and thought that I should tell the truth, because the nun asked me if I was smoking, but I lied, saying that I didn't smoke because I knew there would be hell to pay at home if I got caught. Linda was cool with it. She said that her dad knew she smoked, and she wouldn't get into a lot of trouble. I let Linda take the rap alone.

One day on the way home from school the bus driver, Chuck, stopped the bus and allowed the students to get off and buy ice cream at Carvel on Kirkville Road. I was shocked at this and asked Meg what was going on, and she said, "Well, Chuck is Linda's Dad!!" It was that day that I learned that Linda's mom had died when she was just 11 years old. Meg told Toni and me that Linda had thought that the bus driver was her father, so she and Linda went through the photos and agreed that he was Linda's dad. That morning Tim and Chuck, Linda's brothers, brought Linda to school so they could find out for sure. So that morning when everyone got off the bus, Tim, Chuck, and Linda entered, and Tim asked the bus driver, "Is your name Chuck Kries?"

He said yes.

Tim said, "I would like to introduce myself. I'm your son." Chuck and Linda followed suit. He appeared to be shaken when he realized that these kids were his children. He had not seen them in seven years. When Linda was about 10 years old her mother Irene married Alfonso Sorrendino. Alfonso wanted to adopt Irene's children; they had not seen their father Chuck for a few years at that time. Chuck Kreis was notified that Alfonso wanted to adopt his children, and he let him. So I guess he was trying to make up for lost time; all Linda had to say was that she wanted ice cream and he stopped the bus!

Although they ended up having a relationship with their biological father they always referred to Alfonso Sorrendino as Dad.

Academics

I continued to struggle with academics. I was in the slow math, slow science, and slow English. I was more concerned with having friends than with doing the work. When I would write out a paper, I didn't even know what I was writing half the time, and I don't know how I passed 9th grade!! During this year I continued my aggressive behavior. The English teacher was caring and she noticed my sister's potential, and she was the one who got Toni put into a regular class. Toni wanted to take Regents biology, but the school counselor said no way. Toni didn't do so well in earth science. When 10th grade came she took the non-Regents biology, and she had all 90's and 100's, but again it was too late to be put in the Regents class.

Toni worked hard; she was taking music theory. She said she would get a stomachache because she was so nervous being with the 10th graders. A very good friend in class, Bruce D., talked to Toni, and she took lessons that summer so she could learn the saxophone. She was so excited! She was able to play in the band the next year. One marking period Toni had worked so hard that she was excited, thinking she might make the honor roll. She had 3 A's (one was an A-), 5 B's, and 2 C's. At this point she said she could never be smart like Tina and so many others, because she had worked so hard and still didn't make the honor roll.

Monday, December 18, 1972

One morning Toni and I were in the hall near the library, and we were a little loud. Some of Tina's friends were in the hall with us, and we were talking and laughing, arguing a little over what bands we liked and who was better.

The library nun came out and took Toni and me by the arm and started bitching. Then she let go, and I just walked away as she continued to bitch.

After lunch we had English class. Our Reading/English

teacher was Mrs. Figler. I was sitting next to Tom H., Jim G., and Gigi H; we were fooling around and Christopher was also acting up with us. Mrs. Figler said that I could go into the library for a book.

The library nun opened the door and I didn't have any books with me. Agitated, she asked, "What are you doing coming here with no work?!! Anyway, you and your sister are not to come in here until you bring me your overdue books!" (Toni didn't have any overdue books; she was a good girl and worked very hard). Being twins has its drawbacks—because the teacher couldn't tell us apart, Toni was thought of in a bad light.)

So I said, **"Fuck you!"** I was pissed! I left the library to go to my locker to get the book.

I was in a lot of pain, because I had twisted my ankle on Saturday while I was playing tom tom tackle with my cousins Toni and Jimmy Collins. As I fought the pain I became angry. *My ankle is killing me but no one cares. They don't give a shit.* I walked, and as my thoughts ran through my head I began to feel the pain from Mom's neglect, too. *She doesn't care!! I probably need to go to the doctor for this pain in my ankle. Who cares? I'll play the tough girl!! I can take it!*

I got the book out of my locker and brought it down to the library, which was across from my reading class. I never read the book, and it was the only book I ever took out of the library.

After struggling with the pain in my ankle, I went into the library and was going to set the book on the desk.

The librarian said, **"Give it to me!"** She was very rude and she started with her bullshit tirade. She said, "I'm sick of you kids taking these books and never returning them. I don't know how many have come up missing."

As she was bitching I was beginning to get angry! I thought, *What the fuck? Why is she yelling at me?!!!*

Again she said, **"Give it to me."**

I asked, **"You want this?"**

She reached for it, but I pulled back. She was stunned and reached for it again.

I asked, "So you want this?"

Then she demanded again, "GIVE IT TO ME!!"

I slammed the book on the table.

As I turned to leave, she yelled, "Wait, you have a fine to pay."

I yelled back, "I don't got any money!"

She said, "Don't you raise your voice. You always do this to me!"

I said, "WHAT?!!! I NEVER TOOK A BOOK OUT BEFORE **THAT** ONE."

Then she yelled, "EXIT! EXIT!!!"

So I left and went back into my reading/English class and slammed the door, then my teacher Mrs. Figler came in and called Toni out into the hall. Soon she came back in laughing and said, "I want Mary. I can't get you two straight."

Mrs. Figler said, "You shouldn't answer her *(the library nun)* that way." This teacher Ms. Figler was really nice to me. Then she asked, "Mary, what's going on?"

I said, "Nothing."

"Yes, there is. Tell me."

"Well, she accused me of taking her library book."

Mrs. Figler gently looked at me as though she knew, as though she saw right through me, and she said, "It's okay; tell me what's going on."

I knew that she knew I'd been hurt, and it was as if she knew about Dad and Mom. *How could she know????* She did . . . and she cared. It was the first time anyone cared. I quickly put my wall up tight; I couldn't let her know the truth. *That would be a betrayal and it's not that bad. I can handle myself.*

This was the same teacher who got Toni into Regents English, and she and the new teacher encouraged her and were both there rooting for her on the day of the Regents exam. It was the only one she ever took, and she passed.

Christmas Eve, December 24th, 1972

Mom was angry with me; my cousin Joey was over and he said, "Come on Aunt Judy, Mary loves you." He was sticking up for me, and I was always grateful for that.

During this time we were hanging with kids from Eastwood. I was drinking a lot. It was not uncommon for me to drink a whole bottle of Boone's Farm strawberry wine by myself.

On Christmas Eve we hung out with Aunt Kathy the whole day and night. We stopped for some last minute shopping. We were at the Kmart, and my little cousin Santo and I were looking at stuff and I was keeping him occupied. During the rest of the day we began to plan for the evening, and our friends from Eastwood called and ended up stopping over. Mark and Jim were over; they brought beer and I was drinking apple wine.

I began to drink Jim's beer and I was getting drunk. I was feeling sick, and I got sick upstairs and my brother John was helping me, then I was sick on the stairs. It was not a pretty sight.

We decided to attend midnight mass at Blessed Sacrament. Normally I would have gone to St Peter's or St. Vincent's, but we were hanging with the gang from Eastwood. Toni and I went to church, and I was so intoxicated that I couldn't walk a straight line.

Toni was upset that I went into church drunk, and that I left a few times during the mass to go outside and talk with the guys. Toni would not drink. She would take care of me because it was not legal for us to drink at 16 years old.

The end of 1972, December 31, New Year's Eve, was a wild night. Three Dog Night was on the TV. Some of our friends were smoking pot. I was tempted but I refused.

April 30, 1973

I had a few incidents at school. One day while in the audio-visual room with Meg and Toni, I was feeling impatient. I wasn't going to do any work, and so I wished I hadn't gone with them to view the assignment. *Okay, I know that I have to do this work if I want to get out of 9th grade, but this is stupid.* Toni, Meg, and I looked around and they took out the video and we checked out at the desk.

As I walked out the nun came after us. (I believed that she wanted to fight me.) She yelled, "Stop right there!"

We stopped, and she approached me and asked, "What do you have there?"

"Nothing."

"Yes you do!"

My anger was beginning to rise and I could feel the adrenaline. I said, "BACK OFF; I DIDN'T TAKE ANYTHING from your ROOM!!"

She came closer. I looked at the window and I thought, *I can push her right through it!!!!!* I was **enraged, but I did NOT push her.** I held back and did not put her through the window. There were a number of students around the area and they were screaming, "Fight! Fight!"

She did not HIT ME and just stormed off.

I was again in trouble. *I AM NOT A THIEF!! I never took anything from that damn room!!!! It was the first time I ever went in there all year!!!! I must look like a fucking thief!!! I must look like welfare!! It's always the same shit!! Screw this!!!!*

We are different than everyone here. Toni tries so hard to do the right thing, but I just am not good like her. I am BAD, ROTTEN, and all that Mom says is true!!! I stewed in my anger and my walls were up tight!! My sense of self was damaged, and I knew that I would never fit in with these kids or teachers. *Everyday it's something else!! I am the target. I don't know why I'm different, but I am.*

May 11, 1973

A local band was playing at Lincoln Junior High School. Tina was friends with the band members and we had attended many of these dances. She was very good friends with Stan, the leader of the band. So that night Toni, Tina, and I went to the dance at Lincoln.

When we got there, some of the older boys were fighting outside of the school. There were about 10 of these guys who were just ready to cause a problem.

We knew most of the guys and we were talking with them. There was this one girl who had attended St Vincent's with Toni and me. She was hanging with some other girls who also went to St. Vincent's. Not much had changed; they were together in their clique from St. Vincent's.

One of the guys we were hanging with said that one of the girls was a rag (slut). In retaliation she said, "Yeah, the only rags here are the two in front of you" (meaning Toni and me!!!).

I WAS A VIRGIN!!

I became **enraged.**

She ignored me and went into the dance with her friends. One of the guys began to yell, "THERE'S GONNA TO BE A GIRL FIGHT TONIGHT!!" Toni, Tina and I followed suit and went inside to the dance. I saw her on the dance floor and I went after her. I pushed her and asked, "Who are you calling a rag!?" It was minutes before the chaperones came over and broke up the fight; I was then kicked out of the dance. Toni and Tina followed me outside.

I told Toni and Tina to pick me up so I could get in through the bathroom window. Toni reluctantly helped me. I knew I could fit. As they lifted me I could **feel the adrenaline rush,** and I was ready for the fight. I squeezed through the window. I had some concerns because one of the girls who were with her had a reputation of being really tough, but I fought back the fear. **I was ready:** my heart was pounding and the rage was taking over. I immediately went to the dance floor and looked around for a few minutes. When I found her, I began to beat her; she was unable to defend herself. She was crying, and one of the guys from outside pulled me off of her and said, "No, wait until after the dance!"

As I said, we knew the guys in the band and we ended up going backstage with them. That was the end of it.

I never had any problems with her after that day. People knew that I was not to be messed with.

Summer 1973: Going to Henninger High School

I failed 9th grade earth science. There's a shock!!! Who would have ever seen that coming?

I was not alone. My friend Linda Sorrendino also failed earth science. So when I went to Henninger High School for summer school, Linda was in my class. It was a big joke and she would say, "Hi, my name is Duh and I have to go to summer school."

During this time I was marching in the Marauders, the Drum Corp. The problem was that I was in summer school and we had to go away for 10 days for drum corps competition. So I spoke with someone about dropping the science class and taking it in 10th grade. I was told no problem.

I dropped the class and went away for 10 days. I loved the marching band, though it was a lot of hard work. Toni wanted to play horn and I wanted to play drums, but we ended up in the honor guard. It was our first year ever in a Drum Corp, so you have to start somewhere.

I joined the Drum Corp because I liked this guy Al. He was in the band that we followed, and he gave me drum lessons. I liked him a lot, and he led me to believe that we were an "item." He told me he had recently broken up; however, he and his girlfriend were still together. When I figured out that he was still seeing his girlfriend, I was enraged. So I went and told her that last week he was with me on Thursday, and we compared our weeks; he had told her he was giving drum lessons to some guy named Frank then. Well, I was Frank! She was so upset, and he never talked to me again after that incident. I was crushed.

PART III
Better than
Alcohol

made the decision to go to Henninger High School. Well, after skipping school and being suspended, it was mutually decided that I would attend Henninger. My dad was less than pleased with my attendance and grades. Mom was never happy. I entered in 10th grade. Eventually, I had to attend Central Tech for night school for not finishing 9th grade earth science in summer school.

We were living on Elm Street and Toni was still going to BG. Linda Sorrendino and I were at Henninger and Meg and Toni stayed at BG.

I walked to school by myself, going up Elm Street to Hawley Ave. I took the right onto Hawley and often walked on the path in the park. Lincoln Park was a neighborhood park. If it was windy I would not go up the path because it was hard to light my cigarettes. I would walk by my old house at 1200 Hawley and then to St. Vincent's, and I would think about God in the quiet of the morning. How awesome He must be if He can really see me as small as I am in this world. Standing next to the red-bricked church, the high steeples made me feel very small. I would hide from the wind on the side of the church. I would take a long drag from my Winston and think, *Why am I here? What is this life about? There has to be some plan in all of this.*

My cousin Joey attended Henninger so I got to see him often. Tina Bufano also was attending Henninger.

As Toni and I were growing we knew one thing, and that was that we did not want to live like our mom and dad. It was clear to us that they were miserable. Why would anyone live like this? Toni and I would always pray that God would give us a good marriage, because we did not want the life that our parents had. When I decided to go to Henninger, I told Toni that I thought I had to go there to meet my husband. I just had this feeling.

I was glad that Tina and Linda were there since at least I knew someone. I joined the band because Al had told me to— he was the one who taught me drums. So I figured, *Why not?* I joined the band and I enjoyed playing with them. John M. was really nice and encouraged me.

I also took a home economics class. Linda was in my class and Tina. Linda was always talking about her brothers Timmy and Chuckie. Chuckie had a motorcycle and I liked hearing how close she was to her brothers. I always valued my siblings, so it was a trait that I understood and admired.

Meg, Toni and I joined Blessed Sacraments' CYO. Toni and I tried out for the cheerleading, and Toni almost made the Varsity team, but we were on the JV. We were hanging out with a new crowd of kids. One day after the CYO game, this kid Tony, his sister, and a group of us went to Friendly's on James Street up the street from the school. Linda and her brother Chuckie came to the game that night and Linda introduced us. I felt sorry for her brother because he was limping badly. I did not think much of Chuckie but felt bad that he was in pain.

While at Friendly's, Jim says from across the room, "Hey Mary, did you see Sorrendino tonight?"

"Yeah."

"Well, I did that to him!"

"How?"

"Last night we were playing football and I tackled him and he hurt his leg."

"Oh, well don't be so proud. He was really hurt and had to miss work!"

I did not know why Jim thought I would be impressed that he hurt Sorrendino. During this time I was still battling with my demons. The self-inflicted violence resumed and I began to hit myself. There were many times that I yelled at myself and said, "I hate you." Although I was not beating myself up as much as before, I still had this deep sense of self-loathing.

I was of course drinking when I was with my friends who drank, but it was impossible for me to purchase alcohol. The legal age in New York at that time (1973) was 18, and I looked more like 14 years old to some.

There are other stories that I could share about Tina and me getting drunk and Toni taking care of us, and hanging out with our friends from Eastwood. All I will say is that I drank a lot and looked forward to our times together.

★ ★ ★ ★

I was hanging with Linda, Meg and Tina. It was September 1973 and school was just starting. Toni had a guitar lesson in Eastwood at Guitar Studio on James Street. I was talking with Meg and she said, "Why don't you come over to my house and visit while Toni is at her lesson?" I agreed and went to Meg's. She was living with her dad on Marlborough Street not far from Guitar Studio.

I told her Toni would be about an hour. Meg said, "Let's go see Linda." Linda lived at 122 Ashdale Ave., which is two houses away from James Street. On the corner was a Kentucky Fried Chicken.

We got there and the dog, Football, was barking like mad. I was afraid of the dog, but Meg was not intimidated at all.

Linda answered the door and it appeared that Chuckie and Linda were just playing cards. Chuckie began to wrestle around with Meg.

Meg yelled, "Help me Mary!"

I grabbed Chuckie and tried to pull his arm off of her (they were obviously having fun and played like this often). Next thing I knew, Chuckie picked me up and put me over his shoulder. He began to turn around, faster and faster. The room was spinning. I had on my jean jacket and in the pocket were my cigarettes. They were falling out of the pack one by one and Chuckie was stepping on them!!! I was yelling, "Put me down!" Although I was yelling, I was getting a kick out of the attention he was giving to me.

Chuckie was a senior in high school; therefore he was probably my age. He stood almost six feet tall, and he was blond and blue eyed. After he put me down he and Linda began to joke around. She pushed him and said, "I'll teach you to mess around with my friends!"

He said, "I wish you would. I can't seem to make any headway!!!"

Then she said, "What shall I call you?"

He said, "You can call me anything you want: just don't call me late for dinner!"

These two were very different than the people I normally hung out with. One immediate attraction to Chuckie was the fact that he was close to his sister. Although I knew that they were close, this was the first time I had actually seen them interact with one another.

Despite the fact that Chuckie had acne, he was confident.

Linda and I often talked about "who we liked." Well, I was finally forgetting about the boy I liked from the band, and was thinking about Chuckie a lot. My chance with him was slim to none since he was a senior and I was a sophomore. He also had a job, a motorcycle and was flirtatious. He had girls interested in him; I was sure of that.

One day Linda asked, "Mary, who do you like?"

"No one."

"Oh, don't give me that! Who is it?"

"I don't want to tell you."

"What!?"

"I feel funny and I do NOT WANT him to know!"

"TELL ME!"

"NO."

"Tell me. I promise I won't tell him. Who is it?"

"Chuckie."

"Chuckie WHO????"

"Your brother."

"Get out! Really?

"Yes, don't TELL him. Promise?"

After that talk with Linda, I would see him in the hallways at Henninger. He would have a book in his hand and pretend to hit me on the head and I would duck. Sometimes he would try to grab my nose.

I told Tina Bufano that I thought Linda had told him that I liked him. I was embarrassed; sure that he would not give me a second glance. I was confused because he was now flirting with me. I was walking down the hall talking with Tina about Chuckie and asking her if she thought that Linda told him. We turned the corner and there he was. He reached out trying to hit me. I ducked and he missed (on purpose). Tina said, "HE KNOWS!!!!!"

I confronted Linda and asked her: "Did you tell him?"

"All I said was, 'Chuckie, you know my friend Mary?' He said, 'Oh yeah, that Short Shit . . . .' 'Yeah.' He said, 'What about her?' 'Well, if you asked her out she would go with you.' He did not say *anything. No response.*"

When I would talk with Linda, she was trying to figure out when Chuckie and I could meet (by chance/on purpose). She asked, "When do you have free time?"

I told her and she said, "That won't work. He doesn't skip class."

Then Linda suggested his study hall time, but I had gym class then. She told me what hallway he might be in around that time.

I felt nervous and did not want to try to meet up with him. In fact, I went to the hallway one time and was uncomfortable with meeting him "by chance," so I did not stay. I chickened out.

On September 28, 1973, I was walking up the stairs heading to gym class and there he was. He was coming down the stairs and said, "Hey." I was surprised to see him, despite the fact I knew that he was supposed to be around this hallway at this time. He said, "Where are you going?"

I said, "Well, I was going to go to gym class, but if you want to hang out I could skip it." (I could not believe I said it.)

He said, "Okay."

We walked around the school that September afternoon and then sat in the grass. He was so tall I was afraid, and I was not sure why. I guess he seemed so grown up. I had never been sitting with any guy like this. I did not really know him; although we were the same age, he seemed so much older and more mature compared to me.

As the time came for me to go to class, I got up and he put his hand out for me to pull him up. He pulled me down and gave me a quick kiss. I was taken by surprise! This guy was different.

While we walked back into the school he held my hand.

I entered home economics class with Mrs. Elizabeth Moore. Linda, Tina, and a girl named Cam were also in the class. The minute I got in there I was sitting with Linda and Tina. I was so excited, telling them about what had just happened.

The teacher was annoyed and said, "Okay, that's it! Miss Haupt in that corner, Miss Sorrendino in that corner, and Miss Bufano in that corner!" This teacher was so in tune with her students that she finally said, "Okay, now we all KNOW that Linda's brother kissed Mary, so can we please continue with class?"

I do not know if she had planned to separate us that day or our constant chatter made her act. Nonetheless, this was the day Linda was so happy she said, "We can have yours and Chuckie's birthdays together!!!" It was then that I found out that Chuckie and I are just 11 days apart. His birthday is July 25; mine is August 5th.

Chuckie wanted to take me out on a date, but he was unable to borrow a car from Alfonso, his dad. I was extremely nervous and felt relieved when he could not get it. Instead, he said he would meet me on James Street. He lived in Eastwood. I lived near Burnett Ave. at 334 Elm Street. Toni walked with me since she was going to Tina's house on Durston Ave.

As Toni and I walked up to James Street, I expressed my concern that I wouldn't be able to identify Chuckie until he was near us (I was not wearing my glasses and I needed them desperately). Meanwhile, Chuckie was walking down James Street. I had told him that I would be with Toni, and he was nervous that he might not be able to tell us apart, since we are identical twins. He was just hoping that I would say something and he would know.

I recognized his walk . . . from a long way off.

I went to him right away. Chuckie told me years later how nervous he was walking down James Street, thinking "Maybe I won't be able to tell them apart."

It's a miracle that he ever dated me again. The date consisted of walking the streets of Eastwood; we also stopped at one of his friend's house. I was nervous and talked nonstop! Well, Chuckie ended up getting his dad's car and drove me home. He was nice and gave me a kiss at the back door. I knew that if I wanted to see Chuckie again, I would have to introduce him to my family.

Meeting the Family

The thought of Chuckie meeting my family disturbed me. I understand that most teenagers may feel the way I felt. My mom was not just weird, she was narcissistic and she was always complaining, and it was so unnecessary. Mom was a constant complainer. She would say, "No one believes that I'm sick. I have chronic colitis and have had nine operations, and no one knows how much I suffer . . . ."

She was correct! She did not look sick, although she was very thin.

One day Mom would brag that she had to shop in the junior section for her clothes. She would say, "It's hard for anyone to believe that I had twins! Two babies, and my stomach was just like a rubber band; I returned to a junior size."

The next day, she was not getting enough sympathy because she was SO VERY ill! "No one will believe that I'm sick until I'm dead! Then they will know. . . . When people are in wheelchairs they receive recognition because it's obvious. Not me, just because you can't see that I'm sick, but I AM."

The day came and Chuckie entered the home at 334 Elm Street. My dad was home and he was feeling happy when he saw Chuckie.

"Hello, Mr Haupt."

"Well, you're a tall one."

"Yeah . . . ."

"How would you like to do me a favor?"

"Sure."

(He takes out his wallet and asks Chuckie if he would buy him a six-pack of Genesee beer.)

I protested, "Dad, he can't buy beer. He's only 17!"

My dad just looked at him and said, "He'll be okay."

Great. Now he is going to learn fast that my family is nuts! What decent parent asks his daughter's boyfriend—on the first day meeting him—to buy him beer!!!

Chuckie was cool with it and went to the store as requested. He of course came back with the beer. Chuckie could always buy alcohol; no one questioned his age.

Experience taught Chuckie that if he wanted to buy alcohol, he should *not* bring me with him, because when I was with him he was proofed.

My mom was not home that day, so we made plans for him to come over on Saturday. He came over to meet my mom, and he brought his sister, Linda, with him. My mom laid on the charm, telling Linda how beautiful she was. (Linda was a beautiful girl and still is.) Then she began to tell Linda and Chuckie that she should be dead!

"I had nine surgeries and they took everything out, even some of my intestines."

I want to die. What the hell is she doing!!!!! Chuckie and Linda's mom died at age 36 from cancer. Why, why would she say this shit!!! I glare at her and she does not stop!

"Can you believe I had four babies and I still have my shape?"

Chuckie and Linda listened, humoring her.

Great. That's it!! Now they know.

"So where do you work, Chuckie?"

"McDonald's."

"Oh, can you get my girls a job?"

"I think so."

"Please help them get a job?" (She went on and on about how we needed help to get a job.)

Chuckie said, "Okay."

We began to hang out; I was not in love with him but he was fun. He worked at McDonald's on Erie Boulevard. He already had a motorcycle, but soon he bought a car. Once he got the car I was very afraid! I did not want to have sex or do anything like that. I just remember thinking that would be wrong, and I did not trust Chuckie because he seemed so much older than me. *(We were both 17 years old at this time.)*

One day we went for a ride out to some lake—he knew where there were great places to go. I remember kissing him, and his hand got way too close to my breast and I JUMPED. He was shocked; he had never had a girl respond like this. He said he was sorry. He had no idea, and neither did I (at the time), that my past trauma was being triggered from when my dad violated me as a child. I was truly scared to death. I did not want him or anyone else to touch me.

McDonald's

We continued to date, and Chuckie was still working at McDonald's on Erie Boulevard. It was 1973, and there was only one original golden arches in the Syracuse area. Back then there was only outside seating!

My mom wanted Chuckie to get Toni and me a job. Well, it worked and we were hired. This was my first job. Toni and I were trained for the window. A girl named Penny was my trainer; she was very nice. A kid named Bill Wood trained Toni.

I was awfully nervous; anxiety was high. I was afraid that I wasn't able to do the job. The first area of training was the fries, then the shake machine, then onto the window. In 1973 there were no computers and certainly not at this McDonald's. I loved the fast pace and I was really trying to go fast, but handling money was hard for me.

I was slow mentally; I had a difficult time making change. My drawer was short; I was messing up!!!!! I was in trouble!

The owner's fiancé, Debbie, was so very nice. I think that she saw two girls working really hard. We were dependable and we were honest. One day Debbie came in and wanted to meet with me. She took me downstairs where there was a till set up. She explained that I was giving out change all wrong, and she gently showed me how to count back the money.

I was 17 years old and I had been struggling terribly over giving change. Sometimes I would give people three dimes and a nickel when I should have given one quarter and a dime. Suppose an order came to $3.17, and the customer gave me $5.02. I was a mess. I didn't know why he had given me the two cents!!! Panic would grip me and I couldn't think at all!! Sometimes I would give the customer the two pennies back! During this time the cash register did not tell you what the change was. We had to count it back!

As Debbie and I worked together, though, a LIGHT went on. It was so easy! Debbie showed me that she did not want any pennies so she gave me the 2 cents . . . so think $17 - 2 = 15$. Think that the order is now $3.15. Now add a dime = $3.25, plus three quarters (75 cents) = $4.00, plus $1.00 makes $5.00.

The point was to give back the correct change using the fewest number of coins!!!!

This woman was a godsend. She has no idea of the positive impact she had in my life. I thank God that she took the time to put a little extra effort into training me. If I had failed at this job, Chuckie would have known at that point about my cognition problems, and he would *never* have stayed with me. The fact is I was slow, a loser, and I believed that I had a really low IQ.

I did not believe in myself at all. I had no idea that while I was counting back the money my past trauma was being triggered. Anytime I am put on the spot academically I cannot think. My brain feels frozen and I get terrified. It's unbelievable how slow I was.

* * * *

I really enjoyed drinking, and I had plenty of opportunities with Chuckie since he was able to buy the alcohol. We often would go out bowling, and he could buy the beer and bring it back to our area.

I remember the first time he brought me out to Bridgeport to meet his natural biological father, Chuck Kreis (the bus driver). I was not interested in meeting a man who had signed his children over for adoption. Chuckie and his siblings were adopted by Alfonso Christopher Sorrendino after Alfonso married Irene, Chuckie's mom.

Chuck Kreis lived in a trailer and there was always plenty of beer there. The drive out to Bridgeport was very strange for me, driving out to the boonies as far as I could tell. We took Route 298 and went through Rattle Snake Gulch. I was thinking, "Where in the world is this place Bridgeport?" I was amazed that Chuckie could even find it. Being a city girl, it was real obvious to me that I was out of my comfort zone.

Chuckie's father Chuck played country music; I did not like it at all, but I put up with it. Chuck seemed like a nice guy, a lot of fun. He was happy to have his children in his life. I liked Chuck; he allowed Chuckie and me to stay there, and he would take us out to eat. One time we went to Borios and he bought lobster for Chuckie, and it appeared to me that he was trying to make up for lost time. I must say I respected that.

Although I was grateful to know Chuck's biological father, I loved Alfonso. He was a wonderful man and like a father to me. I could talk to him about anything that was bothering me. He always had words of wisdom, and he knew how to help me not to worry about things.

The Spring of '74

It was a hot day and the weatherman was predicting another warm one tomorrow. Linda wanted to go to the beach and asked Chuckie if we could go. Of course we would have to skip school. I was okay with the idea, but Chuckie would not skip impulsively. He would check the weather and then he would declare that there is no school tomorrow!

I met them at school and Linda said, "There's no school today—Chuckie said so. We are going to the beach!!!"

Linda needed my help because her dad was up when she was getting ready for school, and if he saw her with her shorts he would have guessed that something was going on. So we had a plan that I would go upstairs and get the shorts and throw them out the window. We went back to their house on Ashdale. Just Chuckie and I went in; Mr. Sorrendino was there, and he asked why we were there. Chuckie made up something about me visiting with their little sister Tina; she was just four years old. I then went upstairs and I went into Linda's room, and the shorts were right where she had said they were. I quickly grabbed them and went into the bathroom, opened up the window, and threw them out. Then I heard little Tina LOUD AND CLEAR yelling, "Dad, why is Mary throwing Linda's shorts out the window?" She knew that didn't make sense! We got away with it and spent the day at Sylvan Beach.

By November I was still seeing Chuckie, and Toni was interested in Bill Wood, the kid from McDonald's who trained her. One night after work, Toni, Chuckie, Dale Colella, and Joe went out with some kids from work. I told Chuckie that Toni was interested in Bill, and Chuckie said she'd better let him know. Well, that night Chuckie dropped Toni and me off at 2 AM, and then without me knowing it he went back to the party.

The next day Chuckie had to open the store and he began work very early; therefore we would not be able to see each other, because I had to work second shift. I came into work as he was leaving, and he gave me a note written on the back of the order paper. He said that he loved me and that he would love me forever! The note was amazing!

At this time I was thinking, *Just because I'm dating him doesn't mean he has to be the one and only.* But after that note I was smitten. He also said that he hoped Toni didn't mind, but he had told Bill that she was interested in him and that maybe he could ask her to go see Sha-na-na concert at the War Memorial Arena in Syracuse.

Bill said, "Penny already asked me to go with her and I said yes."

Chuckie suggested that he tell Penny what was going on. Bill told Penny and she said to go ahead and ask Toni; she understood. Bill did ask Toni out, and the four of us went to the show.

Chuckie wore a purple-striped shirt and he looked so handsome!!!! I could not believe that he was with me!!!! It was this night that I really fell for him.

We continued to date. We did not fight like other couples that we knew. There were only two things that would get him angry. First, HE HATED THAT I SMOKED. My mom told Chuckie how sick we were as babies. She told him how my lungs were weak and that I should not smoke. The other thing that angered him was my lack of interest in school. I often skipped class and was in constant trouble in a history class, because if students did not do the assigned reading or were late for class, they would get their names on the board. This one teacher would put the student's name on the board and he would say, "You are on board." I, of course, thought that this guy was nuts. I couldn't have cared less if I passed or failed; I had no drive at all. I would meet Chuckie after every class, and he would walk me to my next class, which I would want to skip.

He would get disgusted with me. He could not comprehend my lack of motivation or my hatred for school; he did not want to be with a drop out. He was a senior and I was in 10th grade, and I was just getting by.

We continued dating and working together at McDonald's. Toni was dating Bill Wood and life was good. I had decided that I wanted to marry Chuckie. We talked about being so young and how society does not accept two 17-year-olds getting married. We were getting closer and closer physically. When I was drinking I was not as scared, although I felt what we were doing was wrong.

By May, Chuckie was making plans for his future, talking about going to Onondaga Community College (OCC) for criminal justice. He liked to say that he would be Detective Chuck.

* * * *

In June 1974 we were talking about his upcoming graduation and the Senior Ball. I was so excited I would be going to the ball with him.

It was unfortunate, but I became really sick with bronchitis and the flu. I was out of school for a week and could not go to work. I had a bad feeling. Chuckie was coming over the house to see me but would not stay long. I had my arms around him, and I put my hands in his back pocket and pulled out a paper with a phone number on it. I was really angry.

"Whose number is this?!!!!" I asked.

"No one's."

I knew it was a girl. I was shocked and the pain was deep. I was pissed; the monster in me was resurrecting.

I looked at the number for just a minute or less, but I remembered it. After he left I called and asked if Chuckie was there. The girl said, "No, but he should be here soon. Who is this?"

That's it, we're done. I will not be made a fool of!!!

He denied having another girl.

When I returned to school I met him at mythology class and there was this girl; they were talking and I knew something was going on. I decided to skip one of my classes and see what he was doing on his study hour. I went outside, and there he was sitting in the grass with HER. They were kissing!!!!! I caught them red-handed!!!!!!

I yelled, "You asshole!" He didn't run after me. He was caught.

I was not going to give up going to the ball; I already had my dress and shoes. I knew the only one who could help me was my Aunt Kathy. I found her as soon as I got home. I was crazy with rage. I had decided I was going to beat the living shit out of that girl. I told Aunt Kathy and she said, "Mary, guys do not like girls who are violent."

I said, "Well, she has to know that he was with me. EVERYONE saw us together since September!!!!!! She didn't care!!"

Aunt Kathy said, "Do NOT attack her."

I was so angry. Aunt Kathy knew that I wasn't hearing her.

She said, "If you do go after her, Chuckie cannot know. So don't leave any marks."

Great advice . . . . That is not what I had in mind.

Aunt Kathy said that if I really hurt her I would lose my chance to get Chuckie back. She knew that was the key to making me understand.

At school I began to follow her, and it did not take long before she was at her locker. I went up to her and she was afraid;

I could tell. I pushed her and she hit the locker. Restraining the monster inside of me took a lot of work. I could see me beating the living shit out of her, but I held back the rage.

I said, "YOU WANT HIM!!!" And I pushed her.

No response.

"YOU CAN HAVE HIM AFTER THE BALL!!!"

I walked away, and that was one of the hardest things for me to do. I just heard my Aunt Kathy saying, "Mary, do not hurt her and definitely do not leave any marks on her. You WILL LOSE him if you hurt her.

I saw Timmy, Chuckie's brother, pulling out of the parking lot. I was walking through and I was a crying mess. He called me over and consoled me. He also smoked, and he put a cigarette in my mouth and lit it. He told me that we would have a good time at the ball.

Chuckie and I spoke and he said, "Mary, we're so young; we should date other people." I did not want this to happen. I couldn't stand to think that he was with other girls . . . kissing them and who knows what else. But I agreed to see him and other people. Of course I did not see anyone else. I took what I could get.

The ball came and I went with Chuckie; we doubled with Timmy and his fiancé Sherry. It was at the Hotel Syracuse; I was sick all night, knowing that tomorrow Chuckie was taking that other girl to the picnic. How that pained me.

There were about three weeks left of school and Chuckie was getting out of control. He had his motorcycle on the road, and now everyone knew that we were not together. It didn't take long before one of the girls at McDonald's let him know that she was interested. She was a student at Bishop Grimes, and she had long, dark red hair. He left work with her on the back of his motorcycle; they were going to Green Lakes.

OH MY GOD, he IS serious. The fact is, he can do so much better than me!!!!!! This girl was tall and athletic, a cheerleader at Bishop Grimes. She was nothing like me—a loser, ugly, with

Indian-straight hair. I definitely was not an athlete.

* * * *

We were at work one night and we got off about 11 PM, and Chuckie said he would give me a ride home. I tried to spend time with him, since the agreement was that we would see each other and others. He was hungry and we stopped at Curry's restaurant on the corner of Thompson and Erie Boulevard; it was a cafeteria-style restaurant. We were in line and I was playing it cool. We were talking as if we were still together; we were comfortable with each other. The line was long, and as he looked at me I was so happy to be with him that I had butterflies in my stomach. When he kissed me that night, I knew I would do anything to be with him. That night I went against my core belief system; if I did what he wanted then I had a chance. I gave him an ultimatum and said, "I can't if you are going to continue to see other people."

It was then that he said that he would just date me.

It was strange for me, but I manipulated him to get him back. I was ashamed of myself and terrified that if I got pregnant he would marry me because he would feel like he had to. I did NOT want to force him to do that!

The fear that I might be pregnant tormented me. I could hear my mom saying, "DON'T YOU EVER DISGRACE THE FAMILY." She would say disgrace in Italian. My mom always looked down on others who "had" to get married.

I told Chuckie that I was late and that I might be . . . . He said, "If you are, I will marry you." He began to look into joining the Air Force. He was thinking, "If she is pregnant, we can get married."

I had to mention this fact because of the torment that I suffered at home. First, prior to having relations with Chuckie, my mom would accuse me of having sex. I would say, "I DID NOT." She was suspicious always, though. She never appreciated anything that I did right. *So what else is new?* I would think. *She has no idea how many times I've turned down drugs —pot mainly. She should be happy.*

When I would go out with Chuckie, she would mock me and say he was nothing but a tall drink of water. I don't know if she was jealous or what her problem was, but she couldn't allow me to be happy.

As I found myself a week late, I went to my Aunt Kathy. She said, "Mary, let your mom know after you tell Chuckie."

When I told my mom, all hell broke loose. I told her that we would get married IF I was. She began to call me a slut and a *"buton."* She was coming apart at the seams emotionally. "What will the family say?!!!" She was yelling again about what a disappointment I was and how she wished she never had me! I had put her through hell . . . .

The constant abuse continued at home, and the name-calling was worse than ever. Finally, I found out that I was not pregnant! I had mixed feelings, thinking of how wonderful it would have been to have a baby. Now I needed to tell Mom, Chuckie, and Aunt Kathy. Toni, of course, was with me through this whole thing.

I came downstairs and told Mom the news. She said, "DO **NOT** TELL CHUCKIE!"

I said, "What?!!!"

"Just let him marry you."

"NO, I won't do that!!"

"YES YOU WILL! If you tell him you aren't pregnant, he WILL leave you."

"I will NOT live like that. If he doesn't want to marry me, that's fine. I WILL NOT BASE OUR MARRIAGE ON A LIE!!!!!!!"

Mom yelled, "DON'T YOU DARE TELL HIM!!!"

I called Chuckie and told him that we needed to talk. We got together and I told him I was not pregnant; therefore we didn't have to get married. I also said that if he wanted to end our relationship I understood.

Chuckie said, "We **are** going to get married, but now we can just wait a year." He had to go to work and I went home.

Mom was waiting to see me. "Did you tell him?"

"Yes, I did."

She began to rant like I have seen so many times before. "You are SO STUPID. I know men. He's gone now, and he'll NEVER MARRY YOU. YOU NEVER LISTEN TO ME."

Aunt Kathy came over and tried to calm Mom down. The whole day was hell. *That's fine; she hates me and no man will ever want me now that I'm no longer a virgin. If Chuckie does break up with me, I will accept it. I refuse to live a lie.*

Chuckie came over to the house and entered the war zone. He had never seen Mom like this. She was screaming bloody murder. Chuckie said, "I do NOT have to listen to this. Come on, Mary."

We walked out while the yelling continued. I told him that I had to be honest. Chuckie and I went for a long walk and didn't come back for hours. He said, "Let's go to the other side of Boulevard; they won't look for us there. They'll try to find us near my house." We talked and Chuckie said that he wanted to marry me soon. He still wanted to enter the Air Force.

When we returned, Mom was relieved that I had come home. I think she knew that Chuckie was not going to be pushed around and that he was not going to let me be abused. Aunt Kathy asked, "Where did you go? I looked all over."

That week I was at Chuckie's house and he said, "Let's go and get your ring." I was surprised. *I think he is serious.* "Let's bike," he said, and I said okay. We got on the bikes and he led the way, but I was shaky. I hadn't bicycled in years.

We went down James Street to downtown and made it safely. We went to a jewelry store. We entered and Chuckie said, "I'm interested in an engagement ring."

The sales clerk asked, "How much would you like to spend?" He gave her a figure.

Diamonds were not that expensive in 1974. We looked at a few and I put each ring on my finger. I could not believe that he was buying me a diamond. He was serious. As I tried each one on my finger I thought, *I don't know what the attraction is with diamonds. They're nice but nothing to get excited about.*

Finally the clerk took out this ½ carat and said, "If you would like to spend a little more you could get this one. It's a keepsake." The band was unique. I loved it. No other ring that I tried on could compare to this one.

Chuckie said, "I'll get this one."

"No Chuckie, that's more than you wanted to spend."

"Well, you are the one who will have to wear it for the rest of your life, and you want this one."

I was thrilled. We were set to pick it up in a few weeks.

∗ ∗ ∗ ∗

On August 5, 1974, Chuckie formally proposed. It was my 18th birthday. When I came home, I was so excited to show my family.

My mother said, "You call that a diamond? I can't even see it. I need a magnifying glass to see that ring. You should have seen the one I had! Now *that* was a diamond. I would have him get you a real stone."

I ignored Mom's slams; I didn't care. Maybe she didn't like it, but I loved it! Aunt Kathy was so happy for me; she said it was a rock!

I went to McDonald's; Chuckie was training for manager, and he did not tell his boss that he was planning on leaving soon. I was walking from the front of the store to the back area. My boss, Dale Collea, was there. It was a tight area, and as he walked by I leaned against the wall and he saw my ring.

Dale said, "What is that?!" Before I could answer he said, "Oh, this is your mother's ring. She gave it to you." He was visibly shaken up.

I said, "No, it's from Chuckie."

"What?"

"We're engaged."

Dale said, "Engaged? Engaged to do WHAT?!!!!!" He grabbed my hand and looked at the ring, then he yelled, "Chuckie, Chuckie!"

Chuckie said, "Yeah?"

"You gave her this?!"

"Yes."

"Come with me."

They went for a walk. Dale had concerns because we had just turned 18. Plus, McDonald's was spending time and money training Chuckie as a manager. Chuckie told him his plan.

Dale told Chuckie that he could not keep his secret and he let Chuckie know that he did not agree with us getting married. Dale was about 20 years old at the time and was attending OCC. He was only two years older than us, but he felt like we were just kids and we were making a mistake.

Dale's father grew up with my mother, and Mom told me that Dale's father Stan used to dip her long ringlets into the ink well during class when they were kids. Stan never denied it. I know, because I asked him about it.

Chuckie graduated in June, was engaged in August, and joined the Air Force in September. He left in September for Lakeland, Texas. We planned the wedding for December 21, 1974.

Just before Chuckie left I returned to Henninger. I don't know why I went back to school when I had no intention of graduating. I took a test and my math score was well below 10th grade level. To graduate, New York State required a student to meet a minimum grade standard. I am not sure of the grade level, but I knew that it was embarrassing to have scored as low as I did. I had this awesome teacher, Mr. Reals, who explained math in a way to make it easy to understand.

Although I didn't intend to graduate, I wanted to improve my math level. I worked really hard and Mr. Reals thought that I could do it.

Meanwhile, I was also taking a home economics class called Family Relations; the teacher, Mrs. Horton, was also amazing. She said, and I quote, "Mary, if you do not do well in this course I will lock you in the closet. I could not allow you to get married if you do not grasp this class." This was the first time a class came easily to me. It was common sense. I did very well and passed the last test prior to my marriage.

I wanted to do well in math; the day came to take the exam. I worked really hard and thought that I would pass the test. I went in afterwards, and Mr. Reals was so upset when he told me that I failed, but if I was not leaving in December he could help me to pass. It was too late, and my school career was coming to a rapid end. Failing that test solidified the belief that I cannot learn.

During this time, while I was trying to achieve some academic success, home was a battlefield. Mom was nonstop yelling, saying "HE'S NOT COMING BACK TO MARRY YOU!!! WHAT MAKES YOU THINK HE'S COMING BACK? YOU'LL BE LEFT AT THE ALTAR ALONE. DON'T EXPECT HIM TO RETURN. YOU BLEW IT WHEN YOU TOLD HIM YOU WEREN'T PREGNANT." She began to call me a slut and a whore on a regular basis. I wrote Chuckie daily, and he wrote often.

When Chuckie wrote he would tell me when he would call. There was no call waiting in 1974, so I would announce to everyone, "Please leave the line open; Chuckie is going to call tonight." Mom would mock me: "Oh, everyone stop living; Chuckie's going to call."

One day my Aunt Fay, Toni and Jimmy's mom, was there. She stuck up for me: "Come on Jules, leave her alone."

"Why should I?"

"She's in love."

"She doesn't know what love is."

Aunt Fay said, "I think she does. Leave her alone and listen to her."

I thank God for my aunts who went to bat for me: my Aunt Kathy, Aunt Fay, and I know my Aunt Helen would help me if I needed her. Aunt Sally, my mom's sister, had a positive impact in my later life.

Chuckie sent me money to help me pay for the wedding and to put any extra into the bank. He always told me how much he missed me. He was at basic training and would return when he was done with basic and tech school.

My bridal shower was at Corner House Restaurant on Grant Ave. I entered the room and met Chuckie's grandmother, Helen Wilson. It was that day that I learned she worked at Bristol with my grandmother Antoinette Prince. They were at lunch and were talking about the weekend. My grandmother said that her granddaughter's bridal shower was this weekend, and Mrs. Wilson said that she was going to her grandson's fiancé's bridal shower. They did not realize it was one and the same.

Chuckie wanted to be a police officer, and he did get into the law enforcement program. We anticipated his return to Syracuse on or near December 15th. We did not realize that weekends and holidays did not count. Chuckie left from Texas for New York on December 19th, was laid over at La Guardia Airport, and did not arrive in Syracuse until the 20th. Our wedding was the next day.

December 21, 1974

I woke up to a perfect winter day; the sun was shining, the snow was perfectly white, and it was not too cold. I had Toni as maid of honor, Tina Bufano, and my cousins Anna Marie, Toni Collins, and Michele Prince as bridesmaids, and the flower girl was my sister-in-law Tina Sorrendino, Chuckie's little sister. She was just five years old. Her partner, the ring bear-er, was my cousin Santo Prince. Timmy was Chuckie's best man; Bruce Decker, Joe Libera, Rick Aleo, and my brother Harry were the groomsmen.

The morning was perfect outside, but inside the home was the storm. Mom was again raging, and I was trying to block out everything she said, but she was relentless. "YOU ARE A *BUTON,* A DISGRACE TO THIS FAMILY." She was enraged, yelling because I had sex before marriage and I did not wear her wedding dress, and she was still making statements that Chuckie was not going to be at the church.

My Uncle Sandy, Aunt Kathy's husband, was the driver for me. He had a beautiful Cadillac, and when he came over he said that I looked more like I was having my first communion.

We spent the wedding night at the Holiday Inn University. (Now it's the Renaissance). We did not have a honeymoon in the traditional sense because we would soon be gone; Chuckie was stationed at Hanscom Air Force Base near Bedford, Massachusetts.

We were in our hotel room alone and the phone rang . . . . It was my Aunt Kathy calling; my mother was furious and had Aunt Kathy call because the ushers took all of the gifts to the Sorrendino house on Ashdale. They needed to be at the bride's house (on Elm Street)! Mom was very upset, saying, "It does NOT even look like we just had a wedding." I was horrified that on my wedding night my mom would call me. Who does that???

* * * *

We left for Massachusetts on the Monday after the New Year. Chuckie looked handsome in his uniform. At Hanscom, we ended up staying in one of the transit trailers. I missed Toni and Harry, but I was married and living with my husband far away from Mom. He was in training; soon he would have to work nights. I had anxiety about him working at night; nonetheless, there was nothing I could do to change that fact.

One of the guys was leaving; he had orders and he needed to sell his trailer, a mobile home. He asked Chuckie if he was interested. My husband asked me what I thought, and I said I thought we should look at it. Chuckie's concern was that we would get stuck with it. I thought that we should check it out because if we bought it then we would be making an investment.

Chuckie set up a time for the two of us to look at the mobile home. It was on government property, and all of the people in the trailer park were military. It was a two bedroom with a nice kitchen, and I loved it the moment I saw it! We discussed the idea and then Chuckie made the final decision. He disregarded his apprehensions and carefully thought out the pros and cons. He then made the decision to buy it. Even if he had not bought it, I felt that he had **heard** me and that **my opinion mattered.**

During the time we were waiting for the closing, we were staying in the transit trailer. Chuckie locked the keys in the trailer; he was so aggravated. I realized that he was embarrassed.

I said, "Hey Chuckie, just let me handle this. I'll go to the main office and let them know that I locked the keys in the trailer."

He agreed. I realized that day that the male ego is something that I must protect as his wife.

Soon we moved in and I loved that mobile home. I got some plants and made that trailer ours. Chuckie was a police officer and had to work the overnight shift.

The nights were **torture.** I hated being alone at night. I had this fear that someone was going to break into the house. I smoked Winston cigarettes and drank Pepsi. I would sit on the couch with my Winstons, Pepsi, and a kitchen knife, frozen with fear. I would not go into the bedroom. Fear had a strong hold on me.

The fear of someone entering my home at night **tortured** me for many years. I say tortured, because I was in agony. I do not know how I ever got through all of those years. The slightest noise and I was on guard. The fear was irrational; I was safe but I did not feel safe. There was this sense of impending danger.

While in Massachusetts, we would of course go to the shopping centers. Chuckie loved to look at records. He could look for hours if I had the patience to wait for him. While he saw the fear that I had at night he did not understand, but he was kind to me and would carry me to bed when he came home. When we would go to the store, I was so fearful that I couldn't leave his side! Chuckie began to help me in the store: he would have me leave him for five minutes, then ten minutes. He desensitized me, and eventually I was okay not being right next to him. He had amazing understanding for an 18 year old.

We decided to buy a motorcycle, so we got part-time jobs at McDonald's. Chuckie worked a few days a week for a few hours so we could save for the motorcycle. My schedule was arranged so Chuckie could drop me off and pick me up. I did not drive.

One of the managers used to tease me. He called me a scatterbrain and said that his girlfriend was also a scatterbrain. I was very fast on the window, and it was competitive. I always enjoyed work; it wasn't like school. I was able to succeed, and I felt that I was above average in my performance.

Once a month there was a team meeting on Saturday morning, I had been working there for a few months and didn't make any of the meetings. Toby, who was a team leader, said, "Hey Mary, are you going to make the meeting on Saturday?"

"Well I'll try; it's tough for Chuckie to bring me here that early."

"Yeah, well just remember that sometimes people can have their rate reduced, and you should really make that meeting. They are important."

Our rate was above minimum wage because when the manager called Syracuse to check out our reference, he discovered that we were both respected and loved by our former bosses. Whoever they spoke with gave us an excellent review. So we were hired and given a higher rate.

I started to think, *Oh my God, I thought that I was doing a good job. I thought that I was excelling; my rings per minute were high. What did I do wrong??? There's something* **wrong with me!**

I attended the team meeting—Toby had no idea that she had gotten me so unsettled. Chuckie told me not to worry; he could see how upset I was.

My sense of being in trouble was consuming me. *I always make a mess of everything!! I can't do anything right!!!!!* I entered the meeting and I felt uncomfortable in my own skin.

During that meeting I was SHOCKED. I was given an award for crew person of the month!!! April 1975.

Toby had wanted me at that meeting so I could receive an award, NOT to punish me. I was so grateful; that award meant so much to me. It told me that I could trust myself. I thought that I was doing an excellent job because I was.

* * * *

The fact that I did not drive was an issue with Chuckie. He wanted me to get my license ASAP! I was afraid of failure, though. There was nothing that I could do right, and taking any test kicked up the fact that I am stupid; I didn't think that I would be able to pass the test. Toby let me use her car because we could not use ours, since it was registered in New York State. Toby's car was registered in Massachusetts. I always prayed to St. Jude because my mother said that he was the saint for hopeless cases. One thing I knew was that I was a hopeless case when it came to intelligence.

When I was 16 years old I failed the written permit test the first time I took it. Miraculously, I did pass the written test the second time. My Aunt Kathy would take Toni and me out to practice; she let us drive her Cadillac, which was a beautiful car. I got up the nerve to take the road test and failed it immediately. I pulled out in front of a truck when the brownie told me to take a left. That failure solidified the belief that I might never obtain my license. I gave up. By the time I was dating Chuckie, I no longer had a New York driver's permit. So I took the test for the permit in Massachusetts and Toby let me use her car to take the road test. Thus, the first license that I ever had was from Massachusetts.

We bought the bike and Chuckie quit McDonald's. I transferred to the Bedford McDonald's, which was closer to our home.

We drove home every few months to Syracuse. We put a lot of miles on that little 360 Honda.

In June 1975, Chuckie was put on the day shift. Later that year he was in the investigation department. Working days allowed Chuckie to take some night courses at the local community college.

* * * *

In November 1975, we were excitedly expecting our first son. My goal in life was to be married and be a mom by time I was 20 years old. I was just 19, married and expecting.

Being Italian, tradition was a strong part of my heritage. If we had a son, I thought he should be named after his father, but Chuckie did not want a junior. I immediately thought of my father in law, Alfonso Sorrendino. I loved his name . . . and I loved and respected him. So when we went home for Thanksgiving we told him and the family "the news." I told him how I wanted our son to be named after him, Charles Alfonso. He was adamant, though, and said, "NO, I do not like my name."

I then asked, "What's your middle name?"

He said Christopher, and then explained that it was a family name. I think his mother's maiden name was Christopher. It was settled: our son would be carrying on his grandfather Sorrendino's middle name.

I was given two baby showers, the first in Syracuse at Aunt Kathy and Uncle Sandy's pizza shop on Elm Street. The second one was in Massachusetts with my friends Judy and Sue and the captain's wife in the trailer park. I do not recall her name, but she had a positive effect on me; she encouraged me to breastfeed. She let me borrow a book, so I chose to nurse my son. At this point I did not know that I would have a son. Back in 1976 they couldn't tell the sex of the child. Or, if they could, my doctor never gave me that option.

After reading the book I thought that I should try it, but I was unsure. So I asked my husband what he thought about me breastfeeding the baby. Chuckie said, "If you have a girl and she asks you about it, at least you would have tried it and could give an answer from experience. If you never try, how could you give advice without knowledge?" He was supportive, so I decided to breastfeed my baby.

My bicentennial baby was due July 2, 1976 and was to be born in Concord Massachusetts, but I began to have problems at 32 weeks. I began labor and was dilated 2 centimeters. Charles *Christopher* Sorrendino was born on May 17, 1976, six weeks early. He was 4 lbs. and 10 oz., and he had to stay in the hospital for almost two weeks. The birth was scary: he didn't breath at first, and the nurse froze. My doctor was furious when she did not move. He said there was a momentary delay of oxygen to the baby. I was afraid, and I began to pray to St. Jude, the saint of hopeless cases, to save my son. Once they got him to breathe, they rushed him away and I didn't get to hold him. On the way to my room I saw him in the nursery; he was in an incubator because he was so small, plus he was on oxygen!! He was yellow and jaundiced, and he was under special lights.

High!! This was the first time I had ever felt a high like this. Having him was the best thing that ever happened to me, and I was instantly in LOVE with that precious little angel. I thought, *Oh my God, he is so beautiful!* How truly blessed I was to have such a wonderful son. The nurses seemed to be looking down on me; I didn't know for sure why I felt that way, but I did. Perhaps it was my age. The next morning, Tuesday, when I woke up I felt awful. I was running a fever. Although I had seen my son for a minute after he was born, I didn't get to hold him then. Now they brought me to see him again—he was absolutely beautiful. The nurses were all talking about me in the hallway. One of my roommates said, "I heard the nurses talking about you out there. Sounded serious . . . ."

One of the nurses came to me and said, "Mary, we are going to move you to a private room." I didn't understand why, and I began to cry.

"Well, you're running a fever, and we don't want you to be near the other women or the babies."

I felt like I had done something wrong. The nurse told me not to worry; we would not be charged extra for the room because it was a medical necessity.

It was late Tuesday and the nurse said that my son was doing really well. "Now we have to get you better so you can see him."

The pediatrician came in; he was happy and announced that the baby had swallowed a tiny bit of water!! That was a big thing for this little boy of mine.

My husband came to the hospital every night and kept me company. He stayed late and visited our son.

On Thursday my fever broke and they brought me my son. I wanted to breastfeed him, and when they gave him to me, the two nurses were shocked at how I held him.

One said, "Oh, you must have babysat a lot!"

"No, not really."

"Well, you're a natural." And I WAS a natural. All I ever wanted in life was to be a mom, and now before my 20th birthday I had my first son.

The nurses helped me put him to the breast and I nursed him! I was very modest about nursing, and then I remembered the captain's wife told me not to be ashamed.

I came home first and visited my son at the hospital each day until he was big enough to come home. The doctor said that he had to be five pounds. After 10 days he was growing but not yet five pounds and the doctor let him come home. They trusted me!

I was on cloud nine, and I could not wait for my family to visit and see this beautiful baby.

One of our friends who was very attractive said, "It's true two negatives [referring to Chuckie and me, who she thought were not attractive] can make a positive." Although that statement brought up intense pain from my past abuse, I was so grateful that he was beautiful. It never occurred to me that she was just joking. . . . I felt so unattractive that I was sure she meant it.

Life was good, and my husband *Chuckie* now became *Chuck.* He told me that prior to having our son he sometimes was not all that proud of me. I was a high school dropout and never really pursued my GED. I smoked cigarettes and he hated that I smoked. I told him that I would finish high school as soon as we arrived in our new home. I lied to Chuck: I did not return to school as I said I would, and I did not quit smoking. I did quit smoking and drinking when I was pregnant. However, as soon as I had the baby I was back to my cigarettes. I had no intention of obtaining the GED, but I bought a book and studied. Nothing had changed! I HATED IT! *I CAN'T DO IT! I DO NOT NEED AN EDUCATION TO BE A MOM and a HARD WORKER!!*

One thing that Chuck realized after we had the baby was that I was smart. He began to believe in me. He said that if I had different parents, Toni and I would both have gone on to college. He thought that I had more sense in raising our son than others twice my age.

Even though I did not grow up with a loving mom or dad, I knew what I wanted for my son. I wanted Chuckie to know that he was loved. He did NOT sleep through the night because he was so small. We put the bassinet in our room, and when he woke us up at night I just loved on him. I wanted him to feel safe. I knew at that point that I would NEVER yell at him, saying, "YOU KEPT ME UP FOR A YEAR!" He was helpless and he needed me to care for his every need, and I was grateful to do it. Each stage of his growth was amazing to me. When he first reached for something at three months old, and when he took his first step, he amazed me!

∗ ∗ ∗ ∗

Back in Syracuse, Toni was still living at home after I left in December 1974 after I was married. Toni was a senior in high school attending Henninger; she doubled up so she could graduate in June 1975. Toni had become the target once I left. Mom began to yell at her; now that I wasn't around someone must be the target, and Toni was abused. Being twins, all of the negative statements were directed at both of us. Another way Toni was abused was that she had to be Mom's "best friend." She had been thrown into an adult role since she was young: about 7 years old it started. She had to be Mom's confidante. Being in that role Toni felt loved, and she trusted Mom. But now when Mom got angry she took it out on Toni. Mom didn't like Toni's boyfriend, Bill, so she began to call her names. The abuse got so intense that Toni was planning on suicide, thinking, "There's no use; the truth is that Mom hates me." "She never loved me either, it was all a lie." One day Mom began to kick Toni while she was lying in her bed; she also spit on her. Toni was traumatized. She didn't know what she had done wrong to get the beatings. She came to the conclusion that she was unloved; and that her whole life had been a lie! The emotional pain that she experienced was what brought her to suicidal thoughts. I was not there for her when she needed me the most. I thank God that Harry and our closest friend Tina Bufano were there for her.

Life had changed for Toni. She was dating Bill Wood, and they planned to marry. Bill had already been married at age 17, and he had a daughter named Tamera Faith Wood, born on October 22, 1974. She was about 18 months older than our son Chuckie.

Well, Toni and Bill married on August 14, 1976. Chuck and I came home for the wedding, and I stood up as matron of honor. Tina Bufano was the maid of honor. Chuck was also in the wedding party and he escorted my cousin Toni Collins. That day I let a neighbor watch my son. By the end of the reception, I was so drunk that I could not walk a straight line. I had the nerve to drive while under the influence and without my eyeglasses!!!! I was so out of it I honestly do not know where my husband was at this point.

During this time, Toni was attending OCC for music. She always loved music, and a mutual friend, Bruce Decker, who was in her music theory class, was also friends with Chuck. He had encouraged Toni to learn the saxophone, back when she was in 10th grade. He saw potential because Toni was an A student in music theory. Toni worked hard and eventually did obtain her associate's degree. I was very proud of her.

Back in Massachusetts

We made friends with John and Karen, who were a lot of fun. We would play cards and hang out. They had one son—Littie, they called him. We were hanging out together one day when Karen asked me, "Mary, do you think you and Chuck will be married forever?"

"Yes, I think we will."

"You're living in a dream world!"

I asked, "Are your parents together?"

"Yes."

"Do they have a good marriage?"

"Yes, but . . . things are different now."

"Well, my parents have been divorced and together. I'm no stranger to bad marriages, and I do not plan on divorcing."

When we got together, alcohol was always a part of our evening. Karen and I were at her and John's apartment. Chuck and John went to buy some beer, and Karen brought me into the bedroom.

She had a joint and she said, "Here, take a hit." I had never tried it, because I was happy just using alcohol.

"Take a toke. . . ."

"Okay." I inhaled and held the smoke in my lungs. I immediately felt the sense of euphoria.

I knew at that moment that I **loved** the way I felt—**no full stomach**, just peace. Time slowed down and music sounded better. *Toni always stopped me from trying this in the past. I have got to let her know what she's missing.* My husband was a cop and he was always a good kid. I didn't think he would approve, so this was Karen's and my little secret.

After that first time, I couldn't wait to go over there again because I wanted to get high. When I went home to Syracuse, I couldn't wait to tell Toni and Harry how awesome pot was.

The fact is, they were WAY ahead of me. They were already getting high, and Toni's fiancé Bill Wood was cool with it. He had Acapulco gold and I even smoked some with angel dust. While at home it was party time. I would get together with Tina Bufano and Linda, and we would go out to Uncle Sam's, a club on Erie Boulevard. It was the place to go in the '70s. I would also visit with my cousin Toni Collins . Harry was playing guitar all the time, and he was in a band with Mark and two other guys. The band was called Joining Forces. Harry, his friends, and our cousin Joey hung out in the garage, which Harry transformed into a living room. It even had a fireplace. Harry was dating Wanda D'Elia, Ada's youngest sister.

★ ★ ★ ★

While in Massachusetts, we had a neighbor named David who was a "Christian." He would come over and talk with us about the Bible, but I didn't understand what he was saying. He always wanted to *study*. He was *studying* Corinthians, and he brought over a *study* book to help us understand the Bible. He was Baptist, and he tried to say that I was *not* a Christian because I was Catholic. Now I knew that I believed in Jesus Christ, and I thought that he made some sense, but he seemed a bit over the edge. I came to the conclusion that *David is a Jesus freak.* When he talked about *studying* the Bible, I thought of academics, and if you have not yet figured it out, I HATE SCHOOL AND ANYTHING THAT IS REMOTELY RELATED TO IT. I had no interest; it sounded hard and I was not interested, period.

One day he was running and jumping in the road saying, "I got the calling!! I got the calling!!" I was convinced he was off his rocker. We did not meet with him much after that.

I worked at McDonald's for a few months after Chuckie was born. Chuck was on days, so he would watch our son while I would work a shift at McDonald's. I loved the nights that I would come home and our friends Karen and John were there. They would be drinking and playing cards. Karen would have some weed, and I would look forward to getting high with her. *Hey, a lot of people drink after work, so what is the difference if I choose to smoke weed!* Needless to say, we enjoyed hanging with them.

It was around this time that I met Peter and Jeannie. She was really nice, and she was talking about the job opening at the childcare center on base. She wanted me to go with her for the interview since she was really shy. I talked with Chuck about it, and he thought that I should also interview. He was excited and said, "Mary, you're *great* with kids. I think you should try to get a job there. That way you can bring the baby with you."

I thought, *Why not?* I told my friend that I would also like to interview, and the two of us went together. By the end of the week I was hired to start immediately.

I felt awful. Jeannie wanted that job real bad and instead I got hired.

Things were going well . . . . I was getting high when I could, but just on the weekends and never in front of my son!! The reality was my son was with me when I was getting high, but he was little and asleep, and I didn't think of it as a big deal because he was too little to know what I was doing.

I missed the motorcycle. Chuck drove it to work, but we couldn't ride together. I wanted to ride the motorcycle and I actually took the test for the permit. Cigarettes were inexpensive on base, so a few times I took the motorcycle to the base. (In Massachusetts you could just ride alone once you got your permit.) I went up to the store, and when I stopped I took my time to make sure everything was in place. I got off the bike and it fell on ME. I had forgotten to put the kickstand down. Luckily for me a cop was nearby; he was thinking, "MAN, these kids have got to learn to leave things alone." When he came up to me he was amused to see Chuck's wife . . . . Well, I never did get my motorcycle license.

We decided to buy a new car, a brand new Honda Civic 1977. The day we bought the Honda Civic, Chuck received his orders.

After two and a half years in Massachusetts, Chuck received orders for a two-year tour to England. This meant that we would have to sell the trailer and go to Syracuse for a while. Chuck left in July, but I had to wait for his orders to change. Chuck was an airman, and therefore his rank was not high enough to allow his family to travel with him. That is why he was only sent for two years. We had to wait for him to be a senior airman; then the orders would be amended, and he would be required to stay in England for three years but his family could be with him. Once he became a senior airman, he could send for me.

We returned to Syracuse for a little vacation before Chuck left for England. My family and friends were enjoying Chuckie, who was a little over a year old. He was walking and talking.

He had blond hair and big blue eyes, and I was loving that. At 15 months his eyes changed to a light brown. He had bright eyes and he was very happy.

When Chuck left in July, I knew that Chuckie would miss him. We had a party at Chuck's family's house, and we all went to the airport to see him off.

From July to September I smoked **a lot** of weed; I was drinking and going out to the club Uncle Sam's on Erie Boulevard. I even brought my younger cousin Tammy with us one night. I was not being a responsible parent, leaving Chuckie with my family. When it came to drugs I was a risk taker. I would use whatever was offered; it didn't matter. I needed to smoke to get some **peace** in my life.

I realized that I was late . . . AND I learned that I was pregnant. I was excited about it. But I then **had** to stop the drinking, the weed, and the occasional speed, and get to a doctor. I almost lost my son Chuckie, and I didn't smoke cigarettes or use drugs during the pregnancy. So I knew that for me, use of any substance was not an option. I stopped and it was a struggle, but I just was not willing to risk any more use. As it was, I had been getting high while I was pregnant; I just did not know it at the time!

One of the most awesome things about Chuck is that he considers my opinion. When we got the orders to England it was the day we bought the new Honda Civic. I said that we should bring it to England, but Chuck did not want to mess with all of the red tape. I was up for the challenge. I made the necessary contacts and learned that the car would be shipped from New Jersey from the port of Bayonne, and we decided to bring the Civic with us to England.

Chuck had again included me in a major decision, but I had to take the car to Bayonne. My dad, Toni, and Harry came to New Jersey with me to see me off, and Toni rode in my car. First, we had to go to the port to make all of the arrangements to have the car shipped to England.

The next day Toni stayed at the hotel with Chuckie and Harry, while Dad and I went to the base. When we arrived at the base's department of transportation; the lines were extremely long; I was concerned because I had to get to Kennedy airport in a few hours to catch a flight to England. I got in line and I felt dizzy. The next thing I remember is my father and some men all around me; I had passed out. They asked if I had eaten this morning and I said no. It was settled: the men took care of my paperwork while Dad and I went and ate breakfast.

Chuckie and I were dropped off at Kennedy Airport. Unfortunately, my flight was delayed and I had to get some lunch for my son. I was alone in the airport. I went to a bank in the airport to cash the money order my husband had sent me, but they refused to cash it. I should have cashed it prior to leaving Syracuse. I asked for the manager: no help. Then I went to an emergency center and pleaded my case, and a man helped me out. I said, "My husband is in the military." I showed him the orders and my dependent card and passport. He cashed the check and I was able to feed my son—not to mention that I was pregnant and also needed to eat. I didn't want to pass out again like I did in the morning.

Chuckie was about 16 months old at this time. His father had left two months before, and I hoped Chuckie would remember him. We flew out of Kennedy Airport and landed at Heathrow Airport. Wow, what an experience! Although I had stopped smoking weed and drinking I continued to smoke cigarettes; I decided that once I got to England I would stop smoking. I had my last cigarette on the plane. *(In 1977 you could smoke while in flight.)* Chuckie was an angel and received a lot of attention. I could bring him anywhere. While on the plane he just sat with me.

Chuck met us at the airport. Chuckie was so happy to see his dad!!! We drove from London to Bodicote Chase, 70 miles outside of London. We lived at 18 Elton Road, an A-frame house. I was so very happy to be with Chuck, but I was home-sick for the US—and for Toni and Harry, of course.

Being a police officer in the Air Force meant shift work for Chuck and nights alone for me. The fear continued to grip me. The fear was just as strong as it always had been. I was in a for-eign land and living off base. But I was the responsible adult, and I had to care for my son! There was not much on TV, and I actually do not know how I made it through that time.

Prior to leaving Syracuse I went to an OB/GYN, and he thought that I should have my cervix sewn so that this baby would go full term. I was leaving the country, so I told the doc-tor that I would follow up on base when I got to England.

I missed my mobile home; we had no furniture, because the trailer was sold furnished. I wished that we had kept the couch. Chuck bought us a bed as well as a little bed for our son. It was a nice neighborhood. Our neighbors were Kathy and David Cuesick. They were great neighbors, and we also became good friends.

Living off base gave me the opportunity to learn the cul-ture of the country. Having British neighbors like Kathy and David was also a key into their world.

Some of Chuck's co-workers, Mike and Laura, were mar-ried, and we began to hang out with them. Laura was a teacher, and they were waiting to begin their family. She was a Baptist and often talked about her faith. She spoke of Christianity in a way that excluded me. *Hey, I know that I'm not perfect, but I also believe in Jesus!!* I sensed a "better than me" attitude, and I had a hard time with that.

She would brag, "Mike and I waited to have sex until we were married."

I just listened.

"My pastor told us not to get into a situation that could set us up for sin."

I just listened . . . knowing that although it was only a few times, I did have sex prior to marriage. *I am condemned.* I also had been taught that it was wrong. Not only was that a part of a religious mindset, it was also a CULTURAL NORM. During the '70s some individuals moved in with each other prior to marriage, and they may as well have had a scarlet letter on their foreheads because that was not socially accepted.

Laura invited Chuck and me out to church. When we went it happened to be on Mother's Day in the UK, so the preacher talked about mothers and how wonderful they are. He spoke of his own mother and of Jesus' mother. My husband was so annoyed. His mom died when he was just 13 years old. I could not relate to what a "mother" is, though I was definitely trying to be what I thought a mom was supposed to be for Chuckie. I never had an example of a good mom. The closest I came to that was when Toni and I lived with Aunt Helen.

Chuck was annoyed and never went back again. I thought that the people were warm, and I wanted to get connected. Laura invited me out again when there was going to be an evangelist preaching; she was really excited. I asked her what the word evangelist meant and she explained, but I didn't understand. She said that he preaches salvation, and I didn't know what that meant.

I sat and listened. The only thing I remember is that the evangelist said, "Jesus said that 'If you acknowledge ME before men, I will acknowledge you before my Father which is in heaven.'" He then asked if anyone wanted to come forward and accept Christ. He said coming forward was a way of acknowledging Jesus before men.

I went forward. I asked Jesus into my heart. I felt good. I never went to that church again, though, because the problems with my second pregnancy began.

I was about five months along when I woke up in the middle of the night. It felt like my water had broken! I also was bleeding! *Oh my God, I can't have this baby now!!!!*

I went down the stairs and called Chuck at work. Linda B. answered; she was a part of Chuck's "flight" shift. I told her what was going on.

"Okay Mary, I put a call out to Chuck, and he'll be heading home soon. Are you still bleeding?"

"No, I think it stopped." I began to cry. "Linda there is no way this baby will live. It's too early."

"Let's not think about that. Where's Chuckie?"

"Asleep."

"Who will watch him?"

"I'll call Kathy next door," I said. "I have to let you go back to work."

"No, not until Chuck gets there." She spoke with me as I waited for him, while he sped home, flying over the hump bridge.

We got Chuckie next door. Chuck brought me to the Banbury maternity hospital around the corner, not far from our home.

The nurse began to interrogate me: "Was there blood?!"

"Yes."

"Was it bright red?"

"Yes."

"Are you sure it was not brown?"

"Yes! I know what color it was."

I was admitted that night.

My son Chuckie was with literal strangers, not having family around to help at a time of crisis.

I was put on bed rest in the hospital. All of the ladies on the floor were pregnant and experiencing some prenatal problem. Upstairs is where all of the women went after they had their babies. However, if the baby did not make it they kept the woman on the first floor, which was a real nice thing to do. Most of the women down on the first floor were having serious problems with their pregnancies; therefore it was possible that their babies might not make it.

Chuck was caring for Chuckie while working full time.

Joyce, the wife of one of my husband's co-workers, took care of our son while he was at work.

When Chuck would bring Chuckie to the hospital to visit me, Chuckie was angry with me for leaving him. He didn't understand that Mommy did not want to leave him; I HAD to leave him.

I was transported by ambulance to Oxford hospital to have an ultrasound done. They confirmed what was suspected: the placenta was in the wrong place. It was low and on the right side of my uterus. It is supposed to be in the upper part of the uterus so it will grow with tissue; being low, there was no tissue for it to attach to, and it had begun to peel off of the wall of the uterus as it grew.

After a week my doctor, Mr. Whitely (in England the terminology was different: the doctors who were specialists were addressed as Mr. and were highly esteemed), let me go home on strict bed rest. He only let me go home because I lived so close to the hospital. I was instructed to call an ambulance if there was any bleeding at all. Mr. Whitely said, "If there is a pin drop of blood, you have to promise to call an ambulance immediately."

"I promise," I said, knowing all too well that if I didn't promise he was not going to let me go home at all.

My neighbor Kathy was wonderful and helpful. Joyce had been a great help caring for Chuckie.

It was weird coming home. Chuck was allowing Chuckie to sit in the front seat of our car, and Chuckie resented that I was home. He was angry with me. He was only 21 months old; his dad had disappeared for a few months, and now I had left him. Although I was uneducated, I knew that all of these transitions had to have some psychological effect on my little boy.

I was home for about a week, and one day the bleeding started. It was more than a pin drop!!! I called my neighbor and the ambulance. Chuckie watched helplessly as the men came in and carried me out. I was glad that he saw I was not leaving him willingly. The nurse who had interrogated me the first time was there; she had made a comment on how I was a Christian and that my behaviors convicted her in some way. The fact is she felt guilty for being harsh with me when I was there last week. She was much nicer this second time.

I was bored and on strict bed rest for a day. Then they let me walk down to the dining room where I would have cereal for breakfast. I am a fussy eater and I have a poor appetite, and the hospital food was not good. No offense, but England is not known for its fine cuisine anyway. So the hospital food with its custard and hot pudding did not set well on my palate.

One evening I was talking with another patient, and she said that she had been there a fortnight.

"Oh, four nights."

"No, a fortnight."

"Okay . . . so you have not been here too long?"

"Yes. A fortnight."

I was so frustrated; I didn't understand what she was talking about. It was hard to understand the accent, but sometimes I did not even understand the language. I did learn that a fortnight is two weeks.

I also was frustrated when the nurse asked me if I had to spend a penny.

"A what?"

"A penny."

"I don't understand."

"Go to the loo."

I was almost in tears with pure frustration. I do have difficulty understanding.

Finally she said, "Go to the toilet," as if she were saying something inappropriate or crude. There were definitely cultural differences that I did not understand until I was living in England.

I had another bleeding episode and I was put on bed rest

again. It happened when I was just at 30 weeks and I was in bed sleeping. I woke up out of a sound sleep and could feel the hot blood flowing. I pressed the call button. The nurse answered and I said, "I'm bleeding."

A few nurses came running, and one said, "We may have to take you to theater (which means the operating room). The bleeding stopped, and the nurse went to call the doctor; she came back and said, "He wants you to stay put."

The next morning my doctor came in to see me. He said, "That's it! You are not getting out of this bed until that baby is born." He meant it.

My husband came to visit me, and the doctor spoke with him and said, "One more episode like last night and I will take that baby. I am NOT going to lose her for that child. If I have to take this baby soon . . . the baby will have less than a fifty percent chance."

Chuck agreed with him. I, of course, understood, but my baby!

I lay in bed. . . . Chuck was home, and he knew first hand that bad things do happen. Chuck's little sister Tina is thirteen years younger than Chuck. While Irene, his mom, was pregnant with Tina, she found out that she had stomach cancer. When Tina was thirteen months old her mom died; she was only thirty-six years old. Chuck was 13, Tim was 14, and Linda was just 11. They all knew about mortality.

The next day was tough. I had to use a bedpan and could not pee! My bladder was bigger than the baby's head.

Later that morning I began to have pain. Contractions! *Oh no, this can't be.* I was in labor. It didn't last long and I had my son; he was 3 lbs. and 13 oz. He was covered with hair and he looked like a lollipop—a head and a stick body!

I didn't get to hold him before he was swept away. The midwives had tried to tell me that when the baby was born I wouldn't be able to hold my baby. They were right: he was taken away immediately. They even had an emergency incubator ready for transportation to Oxford hospital if they thought that he needed to be moved, but he was able to stay in Banbury hospital in their ICU. I was in the hospital with him for a week; I had lost a lot of blood and almost needed a blood transfusion.

We named him Jason. I loved that name. His middle name was after my dad, Harry Lawrence, so he was named Jason Lawrence. My brother Harry is a junior, so he is also named after him. Now Jason was much smaller than Chuckie, and it was painfully evident that this little baby was not ready to be born. As I said, he looked like a lollipop. He couldn't swallow anything, and they put that tube in his nose and down to his stomach. Both his hair and his skin were dark. The nurses asked me what nationality he was. I said, "Mostly Italian," and they said, "No, what else??" I said, "Part Native American." The nurses thought that he looked Native American, but I always saw him as my little Italiano.

I went home after a week. We lived close, so I would visit Jason every day. The nurses did not want me to come up every day, but that didn't stop me; I came up there every chance I could, two times a day. They always had a little blue knitted hat on him and a note saying "please do not feed me, my mum will be here soon." He was so beautiful! I was very proud of him. I wanted to nurse him, but he was being fed by a tube. I would express my milk and they would put it in the tube.

After a few weeks I tried to put him to the breast, but he just did not have the strength to nurse. I continued to express my milk and they fed it to him in a bottle.

He was so small and tired. To get him home I had to give up on nursing, so I did. I had tried and failed. This was an emotional experience, and I felt like a failure; I should have been able to nurse him. My deep sense of failure was resurrected when I was unable to give him the best. The nurses and my neighbor Kathy encouraged me, saying, "You gave him the best when you expressed your milk and brought it up to the hospital. He received the first milk that was FULL of antibiotics." Jason was six weeks old before he came home to live with us.

* * * *

Meanwhile, my husband was flirting with every girl. They liked the attention, and I was getting very jealous.

We were at Bobbie and Preston's home, and we were all drinking when a phone call came in. Preston said, "Chuck, it's for you." I was enraged. ***Who the hell is calling my husband!?***

I took the phone and said hello.

She said, "Chuck?"

Chuck grabbed the phone. He was angry with me.

What the hell is he up to!?

I didn't want to believe that he could be having an affair, but the fact was that some female was calling my husband.

Chuck came home the next day from work with my favorite chocolate: a Terry's Chocolate Orange. He never did that: he was guilty. . . .

I never knew for sure **at this time** if he was cheating, but I had strong suspicions.

* * * *

When Jason was about five months old it was time to get a job. I really liked working with children, so I went to the childcare center on the base and put in my application. I had experience and so I was hired. The love that I have for children is God-given. My mom had no patience with kids. She often bragged, "Kids **always** like me! They are good judges of character." Well, I don't know where she got her information from, but . . . .

I worked well with the children and they liked me. I have never met a baby that I could not calm down. I was able to bring Chuckie and Jason with me to work.

When I was not working directly with the children, I was collecting the money and using the intercom to let the worker in the age appropriate room know that "Darren's mom is here" or "Giana's mom is here." My voice would only go into the room where that child was, not throughout the facility. Jason was little but quick: he immediately recognized my voice and would start to cry he wanted his mommy. It didn't take long for the childcare workers to realize that I was upsetting my son. I loved my boys and I loved being a mom.

Chuckie was great with his brother. By the time Jason was 10 months old, Chuckie knew that there was something wrong. He would say, "Why don't you buy him some shoes? He can't walk because he doesn't have shoes." We did buy the shoes, and Jason crawled until there was a hole in the toe of his shoe.

Jason was trying to talk, and it sounded like he was trying to say, "I want to come up." It was strange. By the time Jason was one year old he couldn't walk, but he said his first word very clearly: ZIPPER. I used to play with the zipper on his PJs. I would put it in my teeth and say "zipper up," and he would laugh out loud.

Eventually the UK stepped in because he was 18 months old and still could not walk. A Professor Tizard and his team saw him at Oxford hospital. It was then that we learned that Jason had cerebral palsy, which can be caused by losing oxygen right after the birth or in the womb. With the malfunction of the placenta, it's not surprising that he has CP. Also, he was on oxygen for a long time, so it could have happened after the birth. Only God knows.

While working at the childcare center, I met a new friend who smoked some pot. I was very interested. She said, "Oh, you smoke?" Everyone knew that I smoked cigarettes, because as soon as I had Jason I went back to smoking.

One evening I was working at the center and she came in to drop her son off. We were talking and she said that they were going to be back late. As we talked, it was obvious to me that she was stoned. I don't remember how I asked, but she said that if I took my break I could go to her house and then come back.

The temptation was more than I can handle. I asked for a break, and then I went to her house and got high. *Oh my God, how I MISSED this.* I pulled the smoke into my lungs and held it in. *I don't know how I went without it all this time.*

I then returned to work stoned. I worked the whole shift, shit faced. The concern was that cannabis/marijuana is illegal; actually, in 1978 it was a felony in England.

I now knew where I could get it, so I did buy from her a few times. I would only use it if Chuck and I were going out to the club on base. Quite often I was unable to get any, so when I got to the club I would start my night off by having a double rum and coke. After two I would begin to feel the effects, and I would then cut back so I could drive home.

Chuck was crazy in those days. I would sit at the table and watch him looking at every other girl in the place. My inferiority was back . . . . *I'm not good enough for him. He can get anyone!* He was six-foot tall with blue eyes and blond hair. He was not a pretty boy, but his personality is what drew women to him. He was funny and fun to be with.

While I was sitting at the table his friends would come over and visit with me. One guy, Mike, was always nice. He seemed so lonely; he was single, as most of our peers were. We were only 21 years old. I liked Mike a lot; he would listen to what I had to say . . . . Meanwhile, where was Chuck? One time he actually left the club for a while and his buddies occupied me. I was naive and didn't want to think that he was cheating on me. I lived in denial.

We often had the guys over and I would cook a nice Italian meal. I'm not that good a cook, but everyone loved my homemade sauce. One day while the guys were there, one of them went outside and I asked my husband, "What's going on?"

"Mary, he's getting high."

I went outside and Pat was smoking hash. Of course I asked for some, and of course I loved the effects.

Well, that was it!!!! Now I liked hash better than weed, and now I knew where to get it and I would never be without it. Pat gave me his number so I could call him.

Chuck wasn't happy; he didn't agree with using drugs! He was a police officer and did not want any part of it.

I thought he didn't want to see me get high because he had never tried it. I wanted Chuck not to mind, so I planned a romantic evening and he did smoke it with me! He was very different than me, though. He liked it, but he didn't care to do it again, and I thought, *How weird!* I could only persuade him to get high a couple of times.

As I've said, I was sexually abused as a child. Chuck and I never talked about it, but I was sexually inhibited. There was a part of me that felt like it was wrong. I'm not saying that I never enjoyed it, but I obviously had some hang-ups.

I asked Chuck not to use the word "relax" and never to say "good girl." It's not as though he ever said those things in the bedroom, but he might tell me to relax if I was overreacting to something the boys did or if I got scared about something. I didn't know it at the time, but that word was a trigger that reminded me of my dad and what he did to me.

Now, when I was high I was not inhibited at ALL, so although he didn't want to get high, there was a part of him that liked the fact that I was enjoying our time together. My inhibitions were gone. Although things were much better, God still had more healing to do in this area of my life.

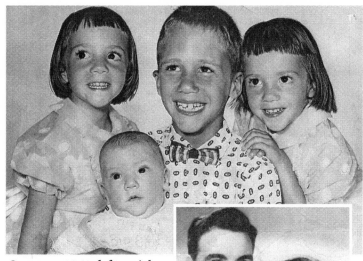

*Summer, 1960; left to right:
Mary, Harry (in front),
John and Toni*

*Mom & Dad,
1955*

1970, left to right: Mary, Harry (in front), John and Toni

2010, left to right: Mary, Harry (in front), John and Toni

Chuck & Mary

Chuck, Mary, Eric, Chuck and Jason, December 1998

Left to right: Eric, Mary, Chuck, Chuck and Jason

"The Breakfast Club," September, 2008:
James Hollman, Mary, Lloyd Mills and Joe Goss.

Left to right: nephew Paul Wood and his wife Aileen,
Chris and Chuck Sorrendino, Chuck, Mary, Toni Wood,
Eric Sorrendino, Jessica and Jason Sorrendino

PART IV
The Gospel

June 1978: We Were 21 Years Old. My boys were a real joy. I loved being a mom and I loved them both so very much. Chuckie was an amazing big brother, very helpful and loving.

I had to wash clothes at the laundromat, and I used the one on the Air Force base in Upper Heyford where Chuck was stationed. I would pile my two boys and the week's worth of laundry into the car and drive to base, where I would meet other Air Force wives.

At this time I was listening to David Attenborough. He was on TV, giving his teaching on the theory of evolution. As I watched the show I was thinking, Maybe he has something here . . . . I was considering that maybe this God stuff is man-made.

I was doing laundry and this woman began to talk to me. She told me that her husband was remote (which means that her husband was away out of the country for a while), and she was all alone with her two children—Tyrone and Nicole. Her name was Gloria; she told me that she also lived in Banbury.

I felt really bad for her, because at this time I was still struggling with being alone at night. I would often have a can of Easy Off Oven Cleaner at my bedside so I could use it as a weapon when and if someone broke into my home. She told me that her phone was not yet turned on. **I could not imagine not having a phone!!!!**

While we were talking, she asked me if I knew the Lord.

Oh no, here we go again. Another "Jesus freak."

"Well, I'm a Christian, if that's what you mean."

She said some stuff and I was half listening. I felt like saying, "HEY if that works for you, GOOD for you!"

I quickly changed the subject and asked, "Where in Banbury do you live?"

She told me.

"It sounds like you're in the same neighborhood as me. I live on Elton Road."

Gloria said, "I know where that is!"

"Well, if you need anything just stop over. You can use my phone anytime." I gave her my address: 18 Elton Road.

A few days later Gloria came to my house and asked to use the phone.

"Of course you can!!"

She **paid** me for the use of the phone. I told her I didn't want the money, but she wouldn't take no for an answer. She used my phone a few times . . . always leaving some change for its use. Once in a while I would see her on base at the commissary or the BX.

Chuck was working nights: three swing shifts, 4 PM to midnight, three midnights to 8 AM, and three days off. The first year this was his schedule, and then he was on days for one year. When he made rank he was put back on nights.

I was becoming obsessed with the hash. I began to buy it from Pat, and he taught me to store it in a film case. I was smoking it out of a beer can, which he showed me how to make into a pipe.

During this time I was working at the childcare center, so we had some extra money. We went out a lot!! When we did a neighborhood teen would babysit.

We were still having parties at the house and now we had drugs. The boys were there upstairs sleeping. It was July 25, 1978, Chuck's 22nd birthday. Pat A. was from Syracuse, so now we had another friend who knew how to play pitch.

During one of our parties Mike was there, and as I said earlier, I kind of liked him. Mike was a really nice guy. Of course I loved Chuck, but Mike gave me a lot of positive attention. I thought that he liked me a lot, but he was a respectable young man and I felt safe.

There were a lot of fields in Banbury, and Mike and I went for a walk. Chuck was angry with me for smoking hash, but Mike was okay with getting high, so we went and smoked together. Nothing ever happened between us and he never told me that he liked me in any way, but it seemed like something was there. I never would cheat on Chuck, because it went against everything I believed in.

This night was just before my 22nd birthday, and I asked Mike to hint to Chuck that I wanted a watch for my birthday. Mike told John and they told me that they were going to buy me the watch.

Chuck was really drunk and left with some of his friends. *AGAIN! Where the hell is he going!!!??*

He said to Mike, "Do whatever you want to with her. We'll be gone for a few hours." I couldn't believe what I heard.

I went upstairs and I lay down and began to cry. . . . I prayed, "God, I never wanted this. All I ever asked for is a good marriage, and THIS is NOT IT!!!" I fell asleep crying and asking God to help me. . . .

In the morning I woke up; Chuck did not come home that night.

I don't know why, but I felt good. The boys were still asleep, which was very unusual because they were my alarm clock. I began to make the bed. There was a knock on the door. It wasn't even 8 AM.

I went down the stairs, wondering who was coming at this early hour. I opened the door and it was Gloria the Jesus freak!

"Hey, come on in. What can I do for you?"

"Nothing."

"Okay???"

"Mary, God has **pressed you** on my heart today. What's going on?"

I began to tell Gloria about my marriage and how this was not the way I had thought it would be. I told her how Toni and

I always prayed to God for good marriages; we didn't want to live like our parents.

She began to tell me that God loves me so much that he sent his Son to die for me. I said, "Yes, I do believe that."

Gloria said, "So what are you going to do about it?"

I didn't understand what she was saying.

We spent the whole day together, and she had my boys and me over for lunch. When I got to her home I sat on the couch. . . . There was a Bible there. I opened it, and in the front was written "Born again" and a date, "Received the gift of tongues" and a date!

I slammed the Bible closed and thought, *OH MY GOD. This woman is in another world.* I saw something spiritual, and I knew that she knew God and that He somehow talked with her. I know that this sounds crazy, but something was revealed to me that day. I learned that in order to be a Christian I would have to give up everything that was wrong. Surrender! Give up!

I thought about it, and I said to God, "Oh God, I can't do that. I can give up the cigarettes and the alcohol, but there is **no way** that I can stop smoking hash!" I thought it was the only thing that let me have any kind of **peace** in my life. I **loved** getting high, and I was not ready to stop for anything.

In January 1979, Chuck's sister Linda called to tell us that their dad died. I was devastated. I know that we were away from him, but Alfonso Sorrendino was a father figure to me. I dreaded telling Chuck. We had received a letter from Linda just a few days prior to this in which she wrote that Dad was real sick and was on oxygen.

Chuck was very upset. Tina was almost 10, and she now had no father or mother. Her mom died when she was just 13 months old; now her dad had died almost 10 years later.

We flew home for the services. I was a mess; I got very ill physically. Tina was so strong, and she walked with me to the casket at the wake. By the time the morning of the funeral came, I was so sick that my husband had me stay home.

Tim, Chuck, and Linda had a meeting about Tina. Linda was not yet 21, but she wanted to be the guardian of Tina. It was decided, and Linda became Tina's legal guardian.

We flew back to England. Chuck was promoted to Staff Sergeant and was second in charge of his flight. He returned to night shift: three swings from 4 PM to midnight, three midnights to 8 AM, and then three days off.

* * * *

Linda called around June 1979; she was upset and wanted her brother. She told Chuck that she was pregnant and didn't know what to do. She wanted to have the baby in England away from everyone, so she closed up the house at 122 Ashdale Ave., and she and Tina came to live with us in England. My husband had to share guardianship in order to make Tina a dependent.

It was a great day when Tina and Linda came to live with us. I was so happy to have someone else there at night. Although I was able to go to bed at night, I still struggled with the fear.

During the first week, Linda and I were sitting up late and talking. We began to discuss religion. I was used to being the only smoker in the house, but now it was the two of us. My little avocado-green ashtray was quite full as we sat there talking. I began to tell Linda about Gloria, and how one night about 10 months ago I prayed to God for help and Gloria came to my house the next day, telling me that God loves me and wants all of me.

"You have got to be kidding."

"No, Linda, it was amazing."

"What did she say?"

"That to be a Christian you have to give your whole self up! Admit that you are a sinner. Know that God sent His Son to die in your place and ask Jesus to come into your heart, and you will then be born again. I'm not ready for that."

Linda said, "It could have been a coincidence."

"Yeah, but I don't think it was." Then I said, as bold as brass, "GOD, IF GLORIA REALLY KNOWS YOU, YOU SEND HER HERE TOMORROW!!!!" I put my cigarette out! "Well, Linda, we will see."

The next day I didn't think of my demand . . . but around 5 PM there was a knock on my door. I went to get it and there she was—Gloria!!!!!

"Mary, is everything okay?"

"YEAH."

"God has pressed you on my heart today, and I had to come here to see you."

Linda could **not believe it.** The last time I had met with Gloria was about ten months ago when she showed up. I told her to tell Linda about being born again and the stuff she had told me. Linda listened and made plans to meet with her at another time.

Now, anyone with half a brain would at this point have SURRENDERED her life to God. Oh no, not me!!!! Because I said to God a second time, "It all sounds so good and I want what she has, but I **CANNOT stop smoking hash!** I can't imagine my life without my escape. I NEED TO HAVE AN ESCAPE!!" I don't even know why, I just couldn't give it up, and I **knew** it was a "sin." Duh . . . it's against the law!

Gloria came over to our home a few times to talk about her God. I think that Linda went to church with her.

Things were out of control. Linda began to get annoyed with me, feeling that I was undermining her authority whenever I said something to Tina. I didn't intend that at all. Sometimes I thought that she was being harsh on Tina, and I would repeat what Linda had said in a nicer way. I realize now that I was out of line, but at the time I couldn't see or think clearly.

There was also tension between Chuck and me over his sisters. The boys were asleep and the shit hit the fan one night when we were drinking. **There's a shock!** Chuck loved his wine, and he and Linda were drinking. Linda wanted to go out to the club. I thought it sounded like a great idea, but Chuck wasn't happy at all. Linda is very persuasive and I went along with it. I felt stuck in the middle: I didn't want Linda mad at me, and I didn't want Chuck mad. I figured that I could reason with Chuck. With Linda on the other hand . . . not so much. I of course was also hoping to get high. We took off and went to Croughton Air Force Base to the club. We had an okay time. I let Linda drive home, since she was trying to learn how to drive a standard, but I was confused and we took a wrong turn and got lost. I said, "We're lost. Let's turn around and head back to base." Linda pulled too far in while turning around and we were stuck!

Oh shit! She tried to give the car gas and I tried to push . . . . It was no use; the car was stuck! We were stranded on a dark country road around midnight.

Linda said, "Let's hitchhike."

I didn't see any other way, so we did. A tractor tailor stopped and gave us a ride back to base. He did try to grab Linda, but we eventually arrived at the gate and I showed my ID.

Of **course** the guard knew my husband. He said, "What the hell are you two doing?" I told him the story and he called a cab. We arrived home at about 4 or 5 AM.

I told Chuck what happened and he wouldn't say a word!!! I have never seen him so angry. I said, "Let's get some sleep and get a cab in the morning." Oh no! He wasn't listening to me.

He got dressed. I followed him. He got his bicycle out and I got mine. Linda knew Chuck was hot; she had seen his wrath in the past. She knew that I had to go with him, while she, of course, would take care of the boys.

He wasn't talking. *I didn't do **anything** to get him this mad! It's **not** like I cheated on him!!! I was with his sister!*

We bicycled and I prayed to God: "Okay, I know that I

CANNOT give up the hash, but I WILL give up the cigarettes if you will PLEASE let me save this marriage. Please don't have him leave me." I was begging God!!! The thought of losing my husband was something I was not ready for.

I don't know how many miles we biked, but it had to be at least 20. Eventually we got to the car, and Chuck had me drive while he pushed. Once we got the car out, he took the bicycles apart and put them in the car. Then he began to talk.

Chuck said, "Linda is single, you're not, and I do not want you going out to the club alone with her!"

"Chuck, I am so sorry. I didn't know that you were going to get this upset."

We got home exhausted, and I found out that Chuck had smashed his guitar when we left him. Poor Tina witnessed the explosion from her brother. The boys were asleep at the time, though.

We went to bed and made up; we made love and he didn't use protection. I didn't care. I was so grateful to God that we had talked out the situation and made up. "I have to give up the smokes," I promised. "You let Chuck and me stay together, and I will stop smoking cigarettes."

About six weeks later I suspected that I was pregnant with my third child. Chuck was **stressed out** at the thought of me being pregnant. Linda and Chuck were extremely worried about me: I felt like they were thinking I had no right getting pregnant when I knew how hard it is for me to have a baby. I went to the clinic on the base to take the test. (There were no home pregnancy tests in 1979.) It was positive.

As hard as it was for me, I had to stop using drugs and alcohol. I had promised God that I wouldn't smoke cigarettes, so I had already quit them. As for the drugs, I wasn't in recovery; I was just abstinent. I don't know how I did it, but I knew that if I wanted this baby I couldn't take a chance with anything! So I white-knuckled it and DID NOT use.

Still, Chuck was not happy and neither was Linda.

I thought, *I'M MARRIED. WHAT THE HELL? And everyone is looking at me as if I DID SOMETHING WRONG! I don't care. I will love this baby no matter what!*

Chuck now lived with two pregnant women. Talk about stress! I thought that maybe being pregnant was an answer to prayer, because Chuck and I might have separated at this time with all of the stress.

By January 1980, my nephew Andrew Charles (after his uncle Chuck) was born. He was one of the most beautiful babies I have ever seen.

I was on strict orders from Mr. Whitely that I was only to take care of the two boys. "NO housework, JUST care for your sons," he said. "If I suspect that you are doing anything more than that, I WILL put you in the hospital!!!"

GREAT! I am such a busy, active person that it was hard, but I wanted to have a full-term baby—one that I could hold right away. I heard that most women get to hold their babies right after they are born!

Linda returned to the US in March 1980. Tina stayed with us because she was in fifth grade, and we believed it was in her best interest to finish the school year.

Our baby was due May 8, but on April 27 I began to have contractions around 10 PM.

Tina was not feeling good that evening and I was playing Barbie dolls with her. She didn't like to be alone. Now that Linda was gone, she slept in the downstairs room alone.

I said that I wanted to lie down and see if the pain would stop so I could get some rest. Chuck was in bed asleep. Tina crawled into bed with me, and there I lay awake, with Chuck asleep on one side and Tina on the other. My watch glowed in the dark and I was timing the contractions.

By 4 AM on April 28, 1980, I knew that we had to go to the hospital. We called Kathy our neighbor and she came over to stay with the kids.

We thought that this one must be a girl. Well, at 4 PM our third son was born weighing 8 lbs. and 3 oz. Oh my God, he was so big! He outweighed both of my other sons put together! (When I pushed and the doctor said, "There is the head," I thought, *What?? There's more?!*)

I was able to hold him right away. The only problem was that we didn't have a boy's name picked out. I wanted an Antoinette/Toni for a girl or Antonio/Anthony/Tony for a boy. Chuck was totally against it. I have 27 first cousins, and 7 of them are named Toni (Antoinette) or Tony (Antonio or Anthony). Chuck said NO WAY are we going to have another Toni/Tony.

One of Chuck's favorite artists is Eric Clapton, so our third son is Eric. His middle name is John, after my brother John and my husband's brother Timothy John.

Holding Eric right away was wonderful. He seemed so big to me, and I was overwhelmed with his size. This little boy had a dent in his head; I was very worried about him. At this time I knew that Jason had some problems and I prayed to God, "Please Lord, let him be okay." I had also prayed this when I had Jason.

He was born on a Monday, and we came home on Saturday. The day that we came home my husband was having a party. The house was full of his Air Force buddies, and the alcohol was plentiful and the music was loud the way we always liked it. I felt upset about it but I went along with Chuck, knowing that this was what he wanted to do. Usually I also wanted to party, but to bring a baby home to this . . . ? Who does this? Who brings a newborn home to a house full of people drinking and partying? Somewhere in my subconscious I knew that this was wrong. I just did not want to spoil the fun for everyone else.

I was not disappointed having another son; no, I was SO HAPPY to have the opportunity to have a full term baby!!!! He was only 10 days early. I was able to nurse Eric, and he was big, healthy, and strong.

He had these pointed ears that made him look so cute. When he was little, he reminded me of an elf in Santa's workshop. He had the biggest brown eyes and long lashes.

It was now April and we would be returning home in July. I was very nervous about going home. First of all, I just had the baby and I still had the excess weight. I knew that my mom would begin to put me down. After I had Chuckie she said, "I don't know what's wrong with you. My stomach was like a rubber band after I had my children. I was never fat. I have a figure like a young girl. I still fit into junior sizes."

I didn't want to hear it!! Linda looked awesome when she left here. So I decided that I would also lose the weight.

I began the diet. Now, I had done this in the past: zero carbs. Well, this time it really got out of hand. I was constantly thinking about my weight. I only ate a small piece of meat for dinner and starved myself all day! I was breastfeeding, so that was not the way to handle this. I also began to jog, running 3–5 miles a day. I was on the verge of a nervous breakdown. I went to the doctors, but the fear of returning home was overwhelming. Although I couldn't wait to get home, the fear of my mom and the fact that I would be living with Linda and in Dad's house was too much!! I knew that my father-in-law being gone was really going to hit me when I got back there.

I also began to binge eat. I am not a big eater, but Chuck was going to take us to London and we planned to stop at McDonald's. I ordered two Big Macs!!! I don't know what I was thinking—I can hardly finish one. I ate them both and then threw up afterwards. I was a mess. This was the first time I struggled with eating problems.

I began to smoke hash again, but I kept my promise to God: no more cigarettes.

Tina returned to the US right after school ended in June.

She took the trip alone and she was under the care of the flight attendant.

Chuck had decided to get out of the Air Force after this three-year tour. He felt that he needed to be near his sisters. We returned to Syracuse, New York, in July 1980. Chuck served in the Air Force almost six years. He got out in July; September would have been six years.

Back to Syracuse

We were traveling with three little ones: Chuckie was four years old, Jason was two, and Eric was just three months old. Our sons were so well behaved, and we received many compliments about how good they were. I was very proud of them.

The flight was a military one; therefore we landed at McGuire AFB in New Jersey. When we exited the plane we were immediately outside. No ramp into the airport. I felt the humidity envelop me; it was so thick you could cut it with a knife. At that point I realized how much I missed the summers . . . . I was home, and I knew that I would never complain about the heat or humidity again.

We finally arrived home in Syracuse, New York, where we moved in with Linda and Tina at their parents' home, in Eastwood. The tables had turned and we lived with them now, although this house was as much Chuck's as it was theirs. The house belonged to all four of the children.

During the day I enjoyed my boys. I would get the blocks out and we used to build a track and drive the little matchbox cars on the wooden track. We would build bridges and I would get the little animals and we would pretend that we were at a safari park. I also would read to them daily. My dad signed them up for a children's book club, and they had a lot of books. The stress was overwhelming, though. Chuck was drinking more and I was getting high as much as I could. Chuck and Linda would hide their beer on each other. I was only getting high after I put the boys to bed.

Chuck was working for a bank as a collector and he hated it. Linda was working in Jamesville as a bank teller. Gram Wilson, Chuck's mom's mother, babysat Andrew.

Concern was increasing because Jason still could not walk. I got in touch with the United Cerebral Palsy center on Court Street. They evaluated Jason and diagnosed him with mild spastic diplegia. He was not yet two and a half and still he could not walk. He had braces on his legs that were fitted prior to leaving the base.

He began physical therapy at the center. He had a therapist named Joanne Barry, who was excellent with him. Dr. Hootnick and Dr. Crossly were the two main doctors we saw at the center.

At this point the thoughts of **use** consumed me. I would go down to my mom's house on Elm Street, because Harry was living there and he always had weed or speed. I was able to get it anytime I wanted. It seemed that I wanted it more now than ever. As I said, I quit smoking the day I promised God. Soon after that I had to stop the hash because I was pregnant.

At my mom's things did not change much; my cousin Joey was around a lot as was my Aunt Fay. It was common for family to come over, and I can hear them saying, "Aunt Judy, you got any Darvons???"

"Sure."

My mom always had something to help family members with the pain. I had no idea that she might be addicted. My Aunt Fay said to me, "I think your mom is an addict."

I wasn't sure about that, but I was sure that she hadn't changed. She continued to bitch . . . .

It wasn't long before I began to smoke cigarettes again. I knew that I had made that promise to God; it was just that I needed them. I began to sneak into the bathroom so Chuck would not know.

Cocaine

Chuck and I were at home with the boys and I was getting them ready for bed. This individual came over to our house to hear the stereo system that I had been telling her about; my cousin Michele was with her. They really liked the system. They left and later this individual returned without Michele and asked if Toni *(Toni had stopped by to visit me)* and I wanted to go for a ride. I knew that meant we would smoke some weed. I checked with Chuck; he knew that I was going to be smoking. The boys were asleep and he was getting ready for bed himself. He said not to be too late. This individual said that she had to stop at a friend's house to pick up something. She invited Toni and me to join her, so we did. That was the first time I snorted cocaine. Oh my God! I was so excited to try it!

Her friends had **a lot.** They made lines on the mirror with the white powder. I was given a rolled up bill. I snorted the cocaine and I liked it. It was great. I found myself staying up all night, and I wasn't tired at all.

Although there was a lot of yelling at Mom's, I continued to go there. I would bring my boys, and we would go visit. I was not going to visit her; I was going to get high. At this point I was getting high when Chuckie and Jason were in another room, and I did not see it as a problem. Eric was always with me and I did not consider that he may be in danger from the second hand smoke.

I lost myself. When I wasn't high I was thinking about it. It happened without me realizing, and I didn't make an effort to avoid it.

At my mom's, Harry and I were in the living room talking and smoking a joint. My son Chuckie used to call my cigarettes rah-rahs. He was just four years old, and he asked me, "Mommy, why are you sharing your rah-rah with Uncle Harry?" He had never seen me get high in front of him.

"Chuckie, it's good to share. We're sharing."

His big, brown, innocent eyes smiled and he said, "Oh . . . ."

At that moment I didn't feel anything. I didn't think it was a big deal at all. I had fallen so far away from my core belief system that nothing really mattered to me. As long as I could get high I was happy.

There was trouble at home with Linda. Although I loved her, we weren't getting along. Living together was draining, and there was constant tension.

My brother John was living at my mom's. He would try to talk to me about drugs. He had a bit of a problem years before and he didn't want me to go down that road.

I'm glad that he cares, but HE is overreacting. It's not like I'm an addict!!!!

Even though my son Chuckie said, "Mommy I want to go to Uncle Harry's room and go on the plane," I just thought that he was cute. It crossed my mind that maybe he was getting a buzz from the weed being smoked in that small bedroom, but I refused to face the truth. I was endangering the welfare of my child.

I was at my mom's house one day. John and I wanted to look at some of our photos that Mom kept in her hope chest, which was in the attic. To get to the attic we had to go into the master bedroom and into the walk-in closet. In the closet were the stairs that led to the attic. John had been listening to the 700 Club recently and felt that I needed to listen as well. He was serious. I had never seen him so concerned about me. As we entered the closet he kept talking . . . so I decided to sit down on the stairs and listen to what he had to say.

"Mary, I've been watching you and it appears to me that you have a drug problem. You're always high when I see you, and you're a mom now and you have to think about your boys."

"You think I have a problem??? John, thanks for your concern, but honestly I'm fine."

"Mary, would you watch the 700 Club?"

"Sure, I'll watch it."

"They talk about addictions and how God can help you stop using."

"Really . . . ."

"Yes."

"Okay I'll check it out."

"Mary, you need God in your life to help you."

"John, what about you? If I need Him, I think you do too."

"No, I'm okay. I'm not using drugs and I haven't in a long time."

I did turn on the 700 Club a few times, just so I could tell my big brother that I watched it.

The summer was great. It was wonderful being back in the States where by 7 AM it could be close to 80 degrees.

Going to my mom's house was difficult, and I realized that I couldn't continue to go there to get high. I had to buy some weed for myself. One day my cousin needed a ride to buy some weed, so I took him to a street off of Burnet and waited in the car. I asked him to buy some for me and I gave him some money.

Now when I was on Ashdale, I could just go for a walk and get high. I didn't have to go visit my mom. I would call my sister and she would stop over, and I would go for a walk and get high; while she stayed at the house with the boys.

Chuck was working at a bank as a bill collector, and he hated it. He said, "If I wanted a job like this I should just be a cop."

He heard from Toni's husband Bill and my brother John that he might be able to get a job at Dairylea on Burnet Ave. Bill worked there and got John a job there as well. Now there was an opening in the cooler. It's hard work, but the pay was much better than the bank and we needed it. Chuck was hired and began his time in the union. He was, of course, on shift work.

One nice thing about living with Chuck's sisters was that there was always an adult in the house. Even though Tina was just 12, I felt safe. On summer nights I could go out and smoke. Toni, Harry, and I went for a walk in Eastwood, and we sat down on a stranger's front lawn. We were stoned and I was picking at the lawn. It was about 12 midnight. I was so happy and comfortable when I was high; I wished I could feel this euphoria all the time. The stress at the house and at Mom's was more than I wanted to handle.

* * * *

Mom never stops . . . . She'll never be happy! I would go down to Mom's to escape the tension at Linda's, and then I would have to face the bullshit at Mom's. It's all shit!! I'm on edge and miserable.

Chuck and I were talking about getting our own place soon: maybe another trailer. My close friend Meg did not want to hear of it. She said, "Mary, you can't get a trailer. They're too dangerous!"

"Meg, what are you talking about?"

"If there's a fire, the trailer can burn up!"

"I know, I had a fire in my trailer in Massachusetts. I'll keep it in mind."

I would live in a shack to get away from the chaos. All I want is some peace in my life. Why does that have to be so hard???!!!

I saw an ad in the paper about buying a home. Chuck and I went to the real estate agency, but the woman was rude and made me feel like trash. "There is no way that you can afford your own home!!!"

Chuck and I were in the Fayetteville office. Of course we couldn't afford a home in that area. I was disappointed, and Chuck and I began to look at trailers again.

I was talking with Tina Bufano, and she said that she had seen an ad in the Sunday paper that sounded like something we might be interested in. I called the number, and the real estate agent helped us. We took a ride out to Bridgeport, which is where my husband's biological father lived. We took 298 east and drove through Rattlesnake Gulch. We put an offer on one of the houses that we saw. It was April 1981. I was busy trying to get the inspections done on the home so we could get the loan.

Between trying to get this house and taking care of my son Jason, I was very busy. Jason was having physical therapy four days a week at the United Cerebral Palsy center on Court Street. Every time I got one thing done, something else would come up. It didn't look like we would be able to buy the home.

During this time not much changed. I was unhappy, and as the months went by I thought that if we could just have our own house, life would be great! It had been years since Chuck and I lived on our own.

August 1981

Months went by, and that August Toni and I celebrated our 25th birthday. We had a big party at Mom's; although she was always yelling at me, I continued to go there. Chuck thought it was strange that I would continue to put myself in the abusive environment. He said he wouldn't talk to my mother if he were me.

I knew that no matter what, Mom is my mother and I don't have a choice. I have to visit her. I could never cut her off. Although neither Toni nor I lived there, we were required to help her by taking her shopping, and that was hell. Mom had to go to several different stores. We would take turns; one week I would take her, the next week it was Toni's turn. When I took my mom shopping, my dad would watch my boys. Dad was living at Mom's at this time. At the checkout, my mother would start to make up shit about me!!! "This is my daughter. She's a social worker . . . ." What the hell is she doing!!! I'm a high school dropout who is dumb as shit! She had to brag about something, so she would make it up.

Also, she would tell perfect strangers that Toni was a music teacher who played seven instruments. Well, Toni had an associate's degree and she did teach guitar to some students. She did play four instruments; saxophone is her main instrument.

I didn't know what was wrong with my mother, but she was bizarre: she would talk to strangers all the time!!! When we were young, we would be in an elevator and she would start to hug us and say, as she showed off her shape, "Can you believe that these girls are my twins??? It's hard to believe that I had two babies!!!"

Mom was a piece of work. Everyone loved her and she loved all of her nieces and nephews, especially my cousin Toni Collins. I don't know why, but she hated me. It was clear to me that she wasn't proud of me and I was a big disappointment.

It's the same old shit. It's now September 1981, and we are still living with Linda. We're getting along, but I want out! I want our own place. Chuck and I **need** our own place. I've given up on that house, but we are still in a contract because we signed the purchase offer and there is a lot of red tape.

I was at my mom's house, and she started to ask me about Jason and Eric.

"You never baptized those boys!!!"

"No, I don't know if I'm going to baptize them."

"What are you talking about?!!! What kind of mother are you?!!! You HAVE to baptize them."

"Well Mom, it's just that I'm not so sure about . . . ."

"If you don't baptize them they'll go to limbo!"

I can't remember everything that she was saying, but as always she never listened. I did something that day that I had never done. I slammed my hand on the kitchen table and said, "WILL YOU LISTEN TO ME JUST ONCE?!!!" I MET THIS WOMAN IN ENGLAND; SHE KNEW GOD, SHE LIVED BY THE BIBLE, AND THAT IS WHAT I WANT!!!! Now show me a baby baptized in the Bible and I will be glad to baptize my boys. You know what I want. I WANT TO LIVE BY THE BIBLE. THAT'S WHAT I WANT."

Harry came into the kitchen and said, "Come on Mary, let's go for a walk."

We went for a walk and got high; the peace came . . . . It always did . . . . I always felt better. The shaking stopped. I was surprised by my reaction to my mom. I never raised my voice to her.

The next two weeks were interesting as I began to think a lot deeper. I was listening to Bruce Springsteen's album *Darkness on the Edge of Town*. There was a song on that album called "Badlands," and I was listening to it with the headphones on, which I often did. I would put the boys to bed and then get high, put on the headphones and just listen to my music. One night I was listening, and though I knew all the words it was as though I was hearing it for the first time. The words were, "I believe in the love that you gave me, I believe in the faith that can save me, I believe in the hope, and I pray that someday it may raise me above these badlands." I played it over and over again, and I asked myself, *What is he saying??? What faith? What can ever raise anyone above these badlands?* I thought, *Is this what Gloria was talking about?*

I began to have some insight into situations in a way I never had. I even asked myself, *Hey what is going on with me? Is it that when you turn 25 you gain wisdom? Yeah, that must be what's going on. Cool.*

On September 29, 1981, I went upstairs to bed. Chuck and I slept in the attic on Ashdale Ave. He was at work. I lay down and I was thinking about all of the stuff I had been figuring out.

I had been listening to Pink Floyd's *The Wall*, and I had begun to understand my dad a little better. He was "comfortably numb." He was drinking his pain away. My mother was terribly abusive to him. She called him names; she used to say that he was a drunken Indian bastard. She also would call him a motion picture asshole. "All he does is sit in front of that idiot box all day!" I began to realize that night that Mom had destroyed him. I felt bad for him and I was amazed at the insight that I was gaining. I had never reflected on this stuff.

Another brick in the wall. *Dad has his walls up. He has to keep the poison out, so that's why he drinks . . . .*

So I continued to THINK about those past few days and how I had gained a deeper understanding of human nature. The dialogue in my mind continued . . . .

WOW, now that I'm 25 and have started to gain some wisdom, so I ask myself what **I could do to get Tina to help me with the dishes?**

I picture myself at the sink alone . . . . I hear everyone in the other room laughing while watching TV. A still, small voice in my heart says, *"if she loved you she would help you."*

I immediately see my broken heart, and I feel the pain of rejection. I feel the pain of **not being loved**. It is as if a knife sliced through my **hard** heart, and I realize at that moment that this insight I've experienced is from God.

I lie there in bed and I ask myself, *What is that prayer that Gloria told me?! Maybe I should get on my knees.* I got up on my knees . . . . I was afraid I wasn't alone. There was something there . . . a presence . . . .

I prayed, "God, I know that you love me. I know that you sent your son Jesus to die for me. I believe that He rose from the dead; and I ask you to come into my heart and take over my life . . . . I AM NOT GOING TO LIVE OR BREATHE UNLESS IT'S FOR YOU. I'M DONE. IT'S OVER." (I meant it! The DRUGS, TOO, I totally and completely surrendered.)

I was not high at all that night. I felt a PEACE enter my heart . . . something that I had never experienced before. It was like I was high but A MILLON TIMES BETTER! I knew at that moment that I would never be the same again.

I heard Chuck come into the house, and I wanted to tell him what had happened. At the same time I didn't want to leave the attic, because I didn't want to lose this presence. I knew that I had the Holy Spirit in me and I didn't want to move, because I didn't want to lose it. I remember at church growing up I heard it said that the peace that passes ALL understanding will rule in your heart today. Oh my God, that is what I had. It was real!!!!

I entered the bathroom and said to Chuck, "Honey . . . I did it . . . ."

"Did what?"

"I did it. I gave my life to God."

"Okay . . . ." (He saw a softness in me that he had never seen. My looks had changed, and he knew something spiritual had just happened.)

"Chuck, I don't ever want this Spirit to leave me."

"Mary, you'll be all right in the morning."

"No! I don't want to be all right. I can't. I don't want to lose this! I **think** that I'm born again! Maybe Toni is too! Being twins . . . ."

I woke up Linda and told her I had done it! I had surrendered my life to God. Linda was gracious to me and said, "Good, we'll talk in the morning."

I knew at that moment I had the Holy Spirit; now I needed the water. I needed to get baptized.

I slept the best I had in years.

THE OLD TESTAMENT
RELIGION

This concept = Man striving to reach God
It is all about works.

God never changes and He said, Sin = Death
Blood must be shed.

In the Old Testament, under the law the people had to bring a perfect sacrifice to the temple and the high priest would offer up the lamb to God as an atonement payment for sin. Man bringing the sacrifice to God.

GOD

I will go to church

I will obey the 10 commandments

I will receive sacraments

I will obey the law

I will be patient

I will be loving

I will forgive

I will not use drugs

I will _____ (you fill in the blank)

I WILL BE GOOD!

MANKIND

THE NEW TESTAMENT
CHRISTIANITY

This concept = God reaching to man!
God sent His Son as the sacrificial lamb.

The Gospel = means the Good News!
What is the Good News? John 3:16. God did it all;
when we ask Jesus into our hearts, He comes in.

It is His Spirit or DNA that enables us
to live a life in freedom and peace

GOD

I am powerless and I have sinned

I came to believe that God loves me
(John 3:16)

I need a Savior

I know that Jesus died in my place

I ask Him to come into my heart and
take over my life

Made a decision to turn my life and will
over to the care of this God (John 3:16)

I choose to live for Him

When we receive his Son we receive
His Holy Spirit, HIS power

In surrender we gain victory by yielding
to His Spirit which is in us

Knowing who we are in Christ,
we are His children

MANKIND

PART V

A New Life

I woke the next morning feeling refreshed and at peace. I was excited and I knew that I had to find a church. I knew what I had experienced was based on the Bible; consequently I needed a church that was based on the Bible. I also knew that I needed to be baptized. I had the Spirit, now I needed the water!

I told Toni on the phone about my conversion, and she was shocked. She was the one who loved God, and it was weird for her to hear me talking about wanting to find a church when she used to DRAG me to church with her as kids.

Toni had to do laundry, so she told me that she would come by my house later. She was going to the laundromat on Teall Ave., so I went to visit with her. When I got there she was all excited.

"Mary, you are not going to believe it!"

"What?"

"I've been talking to this lady who understands what happened to you."

"Really?"

We walked over to where Toni had been folding her laundry, and Toni introduced me to Pat.

Pat began to tell me about God and the Bible. I thought, *Oh my God! She's a Jesus freak! I guess I am too.* She told me about this Bible-based church, and she gave me her business card. I thought, *Maybe I'll go . . . .*

I went home and I felt like God was trying to tell me something. I said, "God, what?" He spoke to my heart and He said, "You asked me where to go; I am telling you."

I immediately pulled out the card from my pocket and called her. I asked her about bringing my boys, and she said that they had a nursery.

Linda came home and I told her that I was going to go to this church. She said, "What are you going to do with the boys???"

"I'm going to bring them with me."

"Oh NO, you're not going to bring my nephews to some strange church; I'll watch them if you want to go with this stranger."

"Thank you, Linda. I really appreciate it!"

It was an evening service about 7:30 PM and everyone was singing. I had never seen anything like it! I noticed this one young girl with her arms lifted to God. It was clear that the same spirit that met me in the attic was here; I could FEEL Him.

A woman named Kathy came up to me and asked if this was something new for me.

"Yes."

"Well, have you ever been to a ball game?"

"Yeah."

"Did you clap or get excited when your team scored?"

"Sure."

"Well, everyone here is praising God for setting them free."

"Oh ..."

"Have you ever read or heard about the Israelites crossing the Red Sea?"

"Yes."

"Do you know what they did when they got to the other side?"

"No."

"After they had seen God drown their enemies?"

"NO."

"Well Miriam, Moses' sister, grabbed her tambourine and began to shout and praise the Lord!!!!"

"That makes sense."

"So you also can praise Him."

"Okay."

That was the first time I went to that church . . . . I learned some good things in the early years, but as the years went on things changed. The experiences I had in that church would take me writing another whole book to explain.

I got home safe and sound that night, and I later talked with Pat about baptism. She said that I could get baptized at that church.

I asked Chuck to come with me to church; he said, "If I'm up I'll go and check it out."

On Sunday, Chuck woke up and he came with me to the 10 AM service. When I would talk with Chuck about Jesus he would always say, "Mary, that's just a crutch, and some people need that."

During the service a lady in the congregation, Sister Royal, was asked to sing. She went forward and sang her heart out. It was amazing! Then the preacher began to speak and all I remember is that he said, "I hate to say this and I never do, **but** some people would refer to the Holy Spirit as a crutch." The Pastor cringed when he said it. "Well, if it is a crutch I'll take three: one for the Father, the Son, and the Holy Spirit."

I knew that God was talking to my husband. That day he went forward and asked Jesus into his life.

Our neighbor and old high school friend Mary Kay Trinca lived down the street. She had "witnessed" to me about Jesus a few times. When I saw her in the neighborhood I called out to her, "Mary Kay! I got saved!!!"

"Really?! I've been praying for you!!! And your family!!"

She invited me to her church, but I was already going to this other Bible-based church, which was close to our home.

Chuck and I got baptized, and Toni and Linda came to the event. Linda and Toni both asked Christ into their lives as well.

By the end of October there was a chance that we might get the house in Bridgeport. At this point, however, nothing mattered. I ONLY wanted God's will in my life, and if I had to stay with Linda that was FINE. I love my sister-in-law; we just had a tough time living together.

The next month the house closed on November 9, 1981, my mom's birthday.

Mom was not too happy at all. She had been bitching about Toni living in the woods. She would mock out Toni and Bill. Mom would say, "Toni and Bill are like Tarzan and Jane! He has her living in the woods! It's a jungle out in Kirkville; their trailer is in the woods! I would never live so far from civilization!"

My mom was furious now because Chuck and I were moving to Bridgeport! The house we were buying was in a residential area; therefore it was not in "the woods." She was trying to control us. She didn't want us to move away and be independent.

November 1981

The first one to welcome me to the neighborhood was Georgia. She lived across the street and she had me over for coffee. Her son Michael was four years old. My boys were five, three, and one, so they had a new friend.

While visiting Georgia I had the opportunity to meet some of my other neighbors. I met Lila, who had about four daughters at the time, and Cheryl Biwer, who I always call Sherry. Sherry lived next door to me but I had not met her until Georgia introduced us.

There were a number of children in my new neighborhood. I did not allow my boys to be outside without me, so often I would be out front with my boys and the neighborhood children. The other neighbors were also outside and we would visit with each other as our children played. I remembered when I was living in Long Island the neighborhood moms would often talk while we played. My mom would never join them; she was different and stayed in the house. I noticed that I was not like her, and I hoped I made my boys feel accepted.

I had gotten close to some of my neighbors, including Sherry next door. In our early years our husbands both worked second shift, Steve at Pepsi and Chuck at the dairy. While we hung clothes out on the line, we would talk over the fence and make plans for later in the day when our husbands left for work. Sherry was eager to hear about the Lord and we had many long talks. She eventually came out to church with me and accepted the Lord Jesus Christ as her Savior.

In our neighborhood we were blessed with great neighbors, including the Mayers, Perollas and the Georges.

Bill was coming out to church with Toni. Back in 1977, on Christmas day, Toni had miscarried in the 16th week. I was in England at the time. Toni's baby would have been 7 months younger than my second son, Jason. It was hard for her, but Toni was taught not to count her chickens before they hatched. So, she just tried to think that it was not a baby and she shouldn't be upset.

Toni got pregnant shortly after she accepted Christ, and I was excited! I thought, *How awesome this is!* Eric was one year old and would be two in April; Toni's baby was due in June 1982. We always thought that we would have our children at the same time or very close in age. Although Jason and Toni's other baby would have been the same age, I was glad that Eric would be just two years older than this baby.

I planned for the baby shower to be when Toni was in her eighth month. That way if she delivered early the baby should be okay. After having Chuckie six weeks early and Jason ten weeks early, I knew how fragile life is.

We had a surprise baby shower at my home and invited a lot of family members. Everyone was so excited because they felt terrible when Toni lost that other baby in the fourth month in 1977. Bill's daughter Tami was there and was also excited, because she was going to have a little brother or sister. Tami was 7½ years old; she was a sensitive little girl.

Tami said to me, "I hope what happened that last time won't happen again."

I said, "Sweetheart, that won't happen. She's almost due ...."
I went over to the trailer where Toni and Bill lived. Bill had put the crib together, and Toni was very excited. But I thought I heard God say that no baby would sleep in this crib **in this house.**

About two weeks later I was sitting at the dinner table and I had this overwhelming sense that something was wrong with my sister. I said to my husband, "Oh my God! I feel like something is **wrong,** like Toni is sick or dying!!!!

Chuck knew how I had had dreams in the past that came true or feelings that had meaning. I immediately called Toni; she was taking a nap, and she was very tired. I asked how the baby was, and she said "Good, but it was weird that the baby kicked really hard earlier." I said I was just checking on her because I was worried. "Don't worry, I'm okay, just tired."

The next day Toni said, "Mary the baby's not moving any more."

"Well, Toni, there's not much room for the baby."

A few days later Toni had an appointment with her OB/GYN, Dr. Ziver Huner. When he went to listen for the heartbeat, there was silence. He immediately asked if she was alone. She said no, Bill had come with her. Then Dr. Huner asked him to come in, and they talked and set up an ultrasound to be done immediately. Toni went for the test and was very confused. As they went down the hall Bill knew what was going on, but Toni was not getting it. She asked Bill, "What are they going to do now to get the heartbeat back?" She said she felt the Lord say that everything would be okay.

She returned to the office and Dr. Huner told her and Bill that their baby had died. Toni was unable to process the information . . . . He offered counseling. Toni said no, she thought that it was WRONG to meet with a counselor because the church we attended spoke against it, and she wanted to do the right thing. At this church counseling was not recommended, and anyone who did see a counselor was somehow in error.

I was home when Toni and Bill left Dr. Huner's office. Bill knew that he had to bring Toni to see me. I looked out and saw them getting out of the car, and I KNEW! God said, "I am in control." I was devastated!!!!! Toni was devastated!!!

I called the pastor's house. It was a Friday, and being Catholic I wondered what they would do to help us. I was recently baptized and Toni was attending regularly. The preacher's wife got on the phone. I was very upset and asked if she knew my sister. She said yes, she had seen her in church. I went on and told her that her baby died and that we would need a pastor or something like that for the funeral arrangements. I asked, "What do you do in these situations?" She said, "Nothing. We do nothing." She never said she was sorry—just "nothing," like it was no big deal! She didn't even say they would pray.

I thought, *Oh . . . this church is much different than what I was brought up in.* I felt hurt by the lack of care and concern for a family in the church that was experiencing a devastating situation. Although this did not make sense, I thought that God had sent me to this church and we were just expected to lean on God. After their response I thought that I was wrong to expect anything from them. I did not trust my feelings or thoughts, so I assumed that I was wrong for contacting them.

During this time my mother's behavior escalated!! She was outraged.

Mom yelled, "NO ONE CARES ABOUT ME!!!!! I'M SICK. I HAVE INTERNAL BLEEDING!!!! EVERYONE ASKS ABOUT TONI JUST BECAUSE SHE HAS A DEAD BABY INSIDE OF HER!!!!! WHAT ABOUT ME?!"

I thought, *She's crazy. We can't take this stress now.*

Mom's rage continued: "Oh, YOU'LL SEE . . . . I'M SICK AND NO ONE WILL BELIEVE ME UNTIL THEY FIND ME DEAD LIKE POOR MARIE, HOME ALONE FOR DAYS BEFORE ANYONE FOUND HER BODY."

I loved Dr. Huner, Toni's Ob/Gyn. (I was also his patient.)

He was a caring doctor and I knew that he cared, so I called him and asked if we could commit her. He said that unless she was a threat to herself or others we could not have her committed. I was so angry with my mom that I thought maybe I should be committed.

Finally, on June 1, 1982 Toni gave birth to her stillborn daughter, Theresa Ann Wood. Toni never went to counseling and therefore was not prepared for the birth. She pretended that she was not going through this. Although she did do some grieving, she never held Theresa. The nurses at Community General Hospital were great. Bill did look at their daughter and said she just looked like she was asleep. She had dark hair, and later Toni found out from the nurse that she had really long eyelashes and she weighed 2 lb. 7 oz. Later in the day Toni asked if she could see the baby now and maybe hold her . . . but it was too late. If she had counseling she would have been prepared for this and would have known that she could have held the baby.

My mom went up to the hospital and created a scene. Grandma was also with her. Of course, now Dr. Huner got to witness the madness first hand. He removed my mom and told the nurses that she was not permitted in the room.

POOR MOM, THE VICTIM ONCE AGAIN!! She cried, "THEY'RE DENYING ME THE RIGHT TO SEE MY DAUGHTER!!!!!"

Toni was traumatized by the event. She worked at a retail store on Erie Boulevard, and many customers asked her if she had a boy or a girl. Toni told them she had a little girl but she was stillborn. The customers and her co-workers were wonderful and compassionate to my sister. It was very difficult working in public with so many individuals having contact with Toni.

* * * *

I was beginning to understand how to parent better. I learned that I was **too** strict. I had the illusion that as long as I didn't beat my children or put them down or yell and say mean things like my mom said, I was doing a pretty good job. I did not see that using drugs around my boys was wrong; that was my world. I never thought that I neglected them when I would go to my mom's house because they were with me.

What I realized was that I put fear into my son Chuckie and that was wrong. I would at times go on a rampage if the toy room was a mess. Chuckie and Jason remember me yelling about the cereal in the closet. After a few of these rampages, they would look at each other and go out into the back yard. My heart still breaks when I think about how that behavior was abuse. Although it would be easy for me to say, "Oh, I had a spiritual experience, and I was then perfect and was the best parent," that is just not true. I had a lot of misconceptions about how to parent lovingly and yet firmly.

I have apologized to my sons for any harm that I may have caused them. My oldest, Chuckie, said, "I was the first child, and you loved the most but knew the least." I thank God that they knew they were loved. God was and is my counselor, and as time went on he began to teach me how to manage my emotions, specifically my anger.

As I went through those early years, I began to feel when I was getting angry before I would explode. I would start to think and say in my mind, "OH MAN . . . OH MAN." Once this thought pattern started, in seconds I was pumped up and agitated.

I was consumed with the house and how perfect it had to be: everything in its place. I don't know how the boys were able to have fun with their toys. My youngest, Eric, used to ask me, "Mommy, can we wash the walls today?" I gave him a small bottle filled with water and he and I would wash the walls, the doors—anywhere there was dirt or handprints. He seemed to enjoy it.

As I continued to be more self-aware I found myself crying. I was normally a hard individual, not one who would cry easily, but every time I thought of the lack of care for God in my life, I felt bad at how I hurt Him and yet He forgives me anyway. I became honest. I started to take a look at the behaviors and the harm that I caused others and God. I did not deserve to be forgiven. I was selfish; I just wanted to get high and I had to see myself as I truly was.

I was going through the very difficult process of facing the truth about myself.

The next thing I noticed is that I have a short fuse. I am supposed to be a Christian, and when the boys would make a mess or get on my nerves I would yell. As these episodes occurred, I realized that I could not go on like this. It was just wrong.

I began to realize that I had to do things differently. I was not always successful, but I began to identify my anger as a test. I had a choice: to allow God to help me or just to have a hissy fit. So when I realized that I was getting tense, my hands would clench and I would be thinking, *Oh MAN!*

"Well, now the test is on," I would say to myself. First, I would make this noise "beeeep" and then say this narrative in my head: *This is a test from your national broadcasting association; this is just a TEST. DO NOT adjust your set. However, in the event of a real emergency you will be directed where to turn.*

I realized that I have a choice to sin or not, to get angry and yell or not. I thought of myself with a choice. I could yield to the Spirit or to the flesh (the brat Mary). The Bible says that we need to yield to the Spirit, so I pictured a yield sign. When I felt the anger rising I would say the narrative about the test, THEN I would PRAY to God and ask for a dose of His Spirit, like a Holy Ghost tranquilizer. When I would do this I could feel his presence, His Spirit, and I felt at peace. It was as though God gave me **His** strength, and in **my weakness** I could be strong through Him.

That was a tough year, being honest to the point of accepting responsibility for my behaviors. I had thought that I was a good mother and now I was learning that I was lacking in a lot of areas, but I was changing.

I would go down to Elm Street to visit my mom as was expected. I would help her by taking her shopping, which was a terrible experience. She was still putting me down. She wanted me to stop reading the Bible; she said that reading the Bible too much would make me go crazy. Mom said, "Mary you have got to stop reading that Bible. When I was in New York City there were crazy people on the corner—Holy Rollers they called them—and you are becoming just like them. You're being brain-washed."

I would assure her that I was okay, but she would only get more agitated. She would yell, "I wish you would go back to smoking pot."

I realized at a young age that I cannot please my mom. During this first year I began to limit my contact with her, because she was negative all the time.

My son Jason asked, "Mom, WHY do we have to go down and see Grandma?"

"Jason, she's my mom and we must be respectful and visit."

"Well, I don't like it there; all she ever does is yell at you the whole time."

I cannot recall **all** of the madness. I do know now that I should not have allowed my mom to treat me like that in front of my boys. She would actually go after me to hit me!!

I remember telling Harry that she went after me one day and he said, "What did Dad do?"

"Nothing."

Harry was pissed!!! When Harry was home he would stop her.

Mom would call me at my home and yell on and on; I was kind of used to it.

One day she wouldn't stop! I would try to hang up, but I

couldn't. So I began to take the phone and set it on the kitchen table. I would begin to wash dishes or fold clothes . . . dust . . . whatever. While the phone lay on the table everyone could hear her yelling. Not because it was on speaker, but because she was yelling at me about something so loudly. My boys were home, and they watched me set the phone down many times *(after that initial incident)* and then pick it up every few minutes and say, "A-HUN. Yeah, okay." I didn't know what I was agreeing to, but it stopped me from filling my life with negativity. I was no longer ingesting her verbal abuse. *(As I think of God as the Counselor, I see that He was teaching me to set some healthy boundaries.)*

In a sense I had believed everything she told me since I could remember. I believed: 1) I was ugly; 2) I was skinny; 3) my hair was too fine—too straight and Indian—and she always said Indian with disdain; 4) I was stupid, below average, and maybe a little retarded, and I say that with **no disrespect** to anyone who may have a loved one with mental retardation as a diagnosis; and 5) I was also BAD, a bad seed like the girl in the movie *The Bad Seed*. My mom did everything to assure me that I was unlovable. She would yell at the top of her lungs, in a rage, "I HATE YOU!!!!" I got the message and put my walls up tight.

I never thought of myself as being abused. There were never any bruises, so I never considered myself as bad off as others.

When Mom would get out of control she would say, "I NEVER HIT YOU!" I would agree: *No, I guess she never did.* Although I had this nagging feeling that she **had** hit me, at this time I didn't *remember* her really doing so.

As time went on and I found myself considering all of the bad things I did to people, I had a sense of profound remorse for my behaviors. I hurt God, yet while I was living my life and not even considering Him I would be overcome with the awe of God. He loved me while I was a mess. I cried a lot this first year as I began to learn of God's mercy and love for me.

I did admit to God and to myself, and I would tell Toni the things that I did wrong. Toni would say, "You weren't that bad; you were a good mom." She didn't understand. But I knew that I didn't deserve to be forgiven.

During this first year I often had drug dreams. In the dream I would be getting high, and I would be so disappointed in myself for letting God down that when I woke up I was relieved and grateful that it was just a dream. The dreams were so real that I thought I was actually getting high!

I stopped listening to all secular music during these early years. At first, every time I heard a song that reminded me of getting high I would switch the station. Then I began to listen to only Christian music.

It was May 1982, and I had been born again / saved for almost a year when I began to have flashbacks. I began to see Mom hitting me and yelling nonstop, pulling my hair. I began to think I was losing my mind. I would be lying in bed and I would envision this torment. Finally I asked Toni, "Toni, do you remember Mom ever hitting me?"

Toni was shocked, speechless for a moment, and said, "Well, okay, so you want to believe that she never hit you!? Well, maybe if you remove 'that summer' then you can say she never hit you, but that would still be a lie."

"WHAT SUMMER?"

"The summer of math summer school, don't you remember?"

"I remember something." (I was remembering her pulling my hair, throwing me against the wall, and punching me.)

"Yeah, she had to drive us to school every morning because we failed math."

"Well, I keep getting this picture of her throwing me against the wall on Hawley Ave."

"Mary, every morning she beat you because she had to

take us to summer school."

It then became clear to me that those flashbacks were real events that happened over and over again.

I asked Harry the same question: if he ever saw Mom beat me.

He shook his head in disbelief and said, "How could you forget?"

I then had this awful anger rise up in me. I knew before that I couldn't stand my mom most of the time. Now I hated her with everything in me. I began to remember so much that I couldn't understand what was happening to me. "Why, God, are you showing me this??"

I called my cousin Toni Collins, now Doran, and told her what had been happening to me. I was hysterical on the phone, and Toni just listened to me sob. I said, "I know that I have to forgive her but I can't." I HATE HER!

My cousin Toni said in a gentle voice, "Mary, you don't have a choice."

I continued to cry. Then I turned to God and cried out loud, "PLEASE GOD, HELP ME!!! I HATE HER!! You LOVE her . . . . If my mom was the ONLY person in this world who would have accepted you, you would have hung on that cross **just for her!!!** You love her so much that you died for her. Please give me just a dot of love for her from you . . . ."

He answered the prayer . . . . I began to have compassion for my mom, and I knew that I had begun to see her with His eyes and heart. My mom was a tormented soul. I called my mom and told her that I forgave her for everything that she did to me. I couldn't say that I had hated her because she would have been devastated. The truth of the situation was that I was WRONG to HATE her and to hold onto that resentment. My mom said, and I quote, "What?! I NEVER did anything to you. I was a GOOD MOM. I never beat you!!!" She didn't have the courage to look at herself and be rigorously honest.

Church

During those early years we had only three stations. Cable TV was available but we couldn't afford such luxury. Besides, at that time the church we attended frowned on cable TV.

One evening I was washing the dishes. The boys were playing and I felt like I had to turn on the TV. I said a quick prayer: "God, if there's some Christian program on, I'll know that you want me to watch it." I went into the living room and turned on the set. There was a Christian program on. It was about a Christian organization called Campus Crusade.

A college student was talking. She said, "I was so angry I pulled my belt out of its loops just like my dad used to, and I began to beat my dorm mate. It was then that these counselors came to me and began to help me understand that I was acting out the abuse that I received growing up. They told me that God loves me and has a plan for me."

I began to cry. "GOD, what is going on?" It brought me back emotionally to the recent memories of my past. The pain that I felt was real. The emotional pain was overwhelming. I was thinking, *Why does this hurt?* **I can't take it.** *I want to just forgive and move on.* I asked God, "WHY ARE YOU SHOWING ME THIS?!!!"

God then spoke to me and said in my heart, "For them." **I knew at that moment that God wanted me to help others who have suffered trauma in their childhoods.** I said, "How am I to do that???? I don't even have a high school diploma." I knew that I would need some education in something like psychology. God said, "Not now, later . . . ."

I was so excited that I scared Chuck; he knew that we were barely getting by financially. He also knew that when I said I was going to help people who have been abused, that meant school, and there was no way we could afford it. I assured him that God said not now later. Our boys were still young and they were my priority; Chuckie was 6, Jason 4, and Eric just 2 years old. I decided then to get my GED.

I was so afraid to take the test; I knew that I would fail it. I made some phone calls and learned that whatever subject I failed I would only have to take that section over again. Then my brother-in-law Bill told me he was going to take his GED. "Why don't we do it together?" So Bill and I took our GED test together on the same day in late June 1982. I remembered some of the science and it didn't seem as hard as I thought it would be. Still, I didn't think that I had passed it. Nonetheless, I was not going to give up. I would just take it again.

Bill passed; he is really smart and I knew that he would pass. I expected to fail, but miraculously I actually passed my GED on the first try!!! I was shocked and thanked God. He did it, not me!!! "Jesus looked at them and said, 'With man it is impossible, but not with God. For all things are possible with God'" (Mark 10:27).

* * * *

We continued at the Bible church; at first our son Chuckie attended the school, and eventually all three of our boys were at the church's private school. The tuition was expensive, but we believed it was what God wanted.

As time went on, God was doing a work in Toni's family. Bill's daughter Tami came to live with them and it was wonderful. Toni adopted Tami; she is 18 months older than Chuckie. Toni and Bill sent Tami to the church's private school as well. It was great to have her there because she was close to the boys, and I knew that she was watching over them. She was maternal and nurturing from the moment I met her when she was just five years old. She took extra care of Jason, knowing that it was hard for him to get around.

Toni did get pregnant again, and she and Bill had a son: William Sheldon David Wood. Tami finally had a sibling on December 9 1983, when she was 9 years old.

I was still haunted by my negative sense of self; I still didn't measure up. I began to teach Sunday school to four year olds. I loved it and I realized that I have a gift. I am a gifted teacher. I also worked in the toddler nursery on Sunday nights.

I hated to miss church; **church** was like my **new drug.** My husband was working at Dairylea on Burnet Ave., right at the end of Elm Street where my mom and dad lived. I didn't know this at the time, but I had a tough time with balance, going to extremes in a number of areas in my life. When Chuck was working the night shift, I still struggled with fear but it was subsiding. I had begun to use that time for prayer. I would seek God and read my Bible. I was asking Him if I could be a good student of His word, not a student like I was in school.

So in the early years I would drive Chuck to work and keep the car on Friday nights. On Wednesdays I would ask a neighbor to drive me. Frank was kind; every time I asked him for a ride he said yes. Frank would say, "This car is my Father in heaven's car, and if I need to drive my sister to his house for a meal I am happy to do it!!" He meant that we were going to church, our Father's house, and hearing the word of God preached, food for the spirit. I would also get a ride from Mary Teresa, a friend around the corner.

I felt bad that Chuck had to miss, but he was on second shift.

I always felt like I didn't fit in . . . . I was second-class. I didn't work at the private school as many of the other women did. Now, some of these feelings were a part of my baggage from the past.

I had a third cousin who also attended this church, but for some reason I felt less than loved by him. Although we were related, I **thought** that he was ashamed of me. The fact is I was ashamed of myself, so I projected that onto him. I also had another third cousin who came out for a short time, Joe, and he was always loving and kind. He actually reached out to Toni and me; I so desperately needed to know that I was accepted, which is why I appreciated Joe. My other cousin had no idea of the psychological damage I had endured. I decided to be proactive: to have friends one must be a friend, so I began to invite some church members over to my home. One individual said, "Mary, don't think that this is going to be a steady thing; you need to find some other people to be your friends because we already have our circle of friends."

I was crushed. *This woman has no idea of the rejection I've suffered most of my life, and now AGAIN I'm damned if I do and damned if I don't. I'm unlovable and unwanted.* I cried out to God and He said, "Keep your eyes on me. I will NEVER fail you!" This sense of rejection was triggering my past; I didn't understand that at the time. However, God counseled me by keeping me in the present. Facing the fact that I felt rejected and hurt was an obvious change in me. Prior to September 29, 1981, I would have kept my walls up. No one would have known that I was hurt!!!!

My husband was independent and never needed anyone. He would reassure me that "everything will be okay; we have each other." I also had my sister, my brothers, and my first cousin Toni, so in a way I had my supports and began to be grateful for them. Toni was playing sax in the band at church and I was teaching Sunday school. I then began to thank God for what I did have, which was: I was close to a few individuals at the church and the ones I worked with in Sunday school.

* * * *

As I was growing in my relationship with God, my relationship with my husband was also growing. When I would go to church and worship God in freedom, I began to realize that God wants me to LOVE my husband, and I needed to tell him how grateful I was to be his wife. During this time, God was healing my inhibitions, and I began to be healed from my past sexual abuse. I began to love my husband with more freedom.

In the past I had confusion from being violated sexually as a seven year old. Prior to this time, I did not realize how that past abuse negatively impacted this area of my life.

I just want anyone who has suffered sexual abuse as a child to know that it was not your fault, and we have a God who wants to heal all of our wounds. If you need to get a counselor to help you through this, I encourage you to do so. It was not your fault. There is hope in our Lord; He is able to heal.

Summer 1986

During the summer of '86, Tina was living with Linda and her husband David in Tully. They had four children at the time: Andrew, Matthew, Jennifer, and Anna Marie.

After discussion it was decided that Tina should move in with us. This was especially hard on Chuckie, who had been the big brother in charge. He was only 10 years old but very mature. Well, now that Tina was living with us, she took on the big sister role although she was the aunt. She was seven years older than Chuckie. Tina was 17 years old and she was going to be a senior in high school the upcoming fall. We talked about where to send her to school, and Chuck and I let her know that if she wanted to go to the church's private school we would pay for her to go. She, of course, was not interested, because she went to public school in Tully and she didn't attend church with us.

During this summer there were (Church) camp meetings. I asked Tina if during the meetings she wanted to hang with her girlfriend from the old neighborhood in Eastwood. Tina thought maybe she would. "Well," Chuck said, "if she wants to go to her friend's that's fine, but I want her to attend one camp meeting, so she can experience it firsthand." Tina was upset but understood that when her brother said something he would stick to it.

She attended the meeting, and she surrendered her life to

God through Jesus Christ. She then knew that she wanted to attend the private school.

The neat thing was that the 12th grade consisted of just one girl and no boys. This young girl was praying to God to give her a classmate so she would not be the only one in the class. Tina was her answer to prayer. Tina's birthday is February 15th and her new friend's birthday was the 16th; they were one day apart.

1984-1986, Worked as a Cashier

Money was tight, and in November 1984 I ended up getting a job at a retail store in Cicero. I started out on the front end. My supervisor was Linda; I was about 28 years old and she was a few years younger. I noticed how professional she was. I saw myself as so much older than she, but I'm sure it was only three years. She often told me what a good job I was doing. I didn't know it at the time, but I was desperate for positive feedback. I always liked to work because I was a hard worker; even when I was at McDonald's I enjoyed work.

As I stated, next door were the Biwers, and across the street were the Bosmas, Gary and Cathie. Now, Cathie and Gary moved across the street a few years after we came to this neighborhood. Coincidently, they also attended the same church. They were an incredible help because working in retail meant that I had to work most Saturdays. With Chuck's schedule— shift work—he was unable to transport our boys to the Saturday activities at the school. The Biwers' and the Bosmas' children all went to the same private school as our boys. On Saturdays there would be athletic activities, and the Bosmas and the Biwers would help with transportation for my boys. This allowed for us to help each other out with car pools. Gary and I taught Sunday school, so we would often ride together.

★ ★ ★ ★

Dad was sick. He had survived open-heart surgery when he was in his early 50s, but now he was getting very sick. I talked with him and he told me that they were going to give him a colostomy bag. I knew that he was facing very serious surgery.

Mom was complaining, "Oh, he has to have surgery! Well, I know what that's like; I had nine surgeries." I said to Mom that this was different because he was going to have a colostomy bag. Mom didn't care and minimized how serious the procedure was.

I took the day off from work so my brother Harry and I could be up in the hospital together while Dad was undergoing the operation. He had surgery on December 8, 1986 on his 60th birthday. I planned to take my husband to work so I would have the car.

Mom called me and said, "There's no need for you to be up in the hospital! I just spoke to the nurse and she told me not to come!"

"Well, Harry and I will be up there."

Mom was angry. She didn't want me up there.

She called me back and said, "I just talked to Harry and he's not going up to the hospital."

"Oh," I said, "I thought that he was." I knew that she had called me in an effort to stop me from going to the hospital, and then she must have called Harry and stopped him. Well, I wasn't going to be there alone all day, so I let Chuck leave with the car.

I found out later that day that Harry was at the hospital ALL day alone. Dad was in surgery for 14 hours, and my brother was alone the whole time because I believed my mom. I should have called my brother to hear from him that he was not going. I believed my mom though I should have known better. That is one of my biggest regrets; I still feel sad for not being with my brother that day.

After the surgery I would go up to the VA hospital and visit my dad. He had a tough time, and he was hallucinating. At night the nurses were tying him down. I visited him as much as I could, and Toni and Harry were up there a lot. When Dad got out of the hospital Harry took care of him. He sacrificed to help Dad. Mom was still yelling.

Toni would also come up to the VA. Her boys were very young; she now had another son named Paul.

By May Dad took a turn for the worse and landed back in the hospital. We weren't getting enough information about his condition.

One Sunday Harry and I were up in his room. Dad was upset because his feet were cold. I had church at 7:30 PM and I needed to get home to get ready. I called Mom because if she was not going to be coming up there later I was going to go to the house to get him his socks. Mom said that she was coming up later and would bring socks. This was the last time I saw my father alive.

I came home from work on Thursday the 14th of May, and my husband was on the phone with Bill. It sounded serious. I asked, "Is Chip okay?" (Bill's brother had been ill at this time.) Chuck shook his head no. I was so upset. I asked, "Is he dead?" Chuck nodded his head yes. I yelled, "OH NO! CHIP!" Chuck then said, "Not Chip, your dad . . . ." There was a part of me that was relieved that it wasn't Chip. He was too young to die, only 32 years old.

Dad died on May 14, 1987. He was 60 years old, he had colon cancer and it appeared that his heart gave out.

The New Department, 1986-1987

Working at the retail store was a big thing for me. I loved the fact that I was able to work and help pay some of the bills. I was asked if I would be interested in working in the candy department within the grocery department, and I jumped at the offer.

I began to work for John, the grocery manager. He explained that he wanted the 12-foot section to look like a wall.

He showed me how it should look. The girls who worked in the General Merchandise department, Susie and Colleen, would ask if I wanted to join them for lunch. I felt that I belonged and was appreciated. It felt good.

Sometimes it seemed that John was angry with me. (The fact was that he was very busy and didn't have the time to stop and show me step by step how he wanted it done. John had worked in the business for years; I was new at it.) Finally I faced my fears and spoke up. I did this on a few occasions and learned that I did not need to be afraid. He was not angry, it was my perception of the situation and my frame of reference that was skewed.

I eventually got into the General Merchandise (GM) department, where I worked with Kevin, Susie, Colleen, and Arlene. I enjoyed it.

Eventually I got a job as the assistant GM manager in Liverpool. It was not full time, but it was a great opportunity if I wanted a career in the GM department. This was a turning point for me, though I didn't know it at the time. My boss was a hard worker, and she knew my sister Toni because Toni had been working in the Dewitt store for four or five years before I began.

My boss had a planned vacation during the holiday week; this was the first time that I would be running the department alone. I knew that I would need help. I asked and got permission to have help on Christmas Eve due to it being a short day. I was able to have my sister Toni come over from the Dewitt store, she also had worked in General Merchandise and would be able to handle the job.

Toni was on the floor working putting up some items and the assistant store manager John D. saw her and he asked, "How are you doing today?" Toni said "Okay, I am Toni" (*This was the first time she had met John D. He, of course, thought Toni was me*), and he thought that I said, "I was tired." John then replied, "Come out back and sit down. We have provided lunch for everyone today." Toni said, "I will have to check with Mary to see if that would be okay." Now John just looks at Toni and goes back into the back area and sees the store manager, Dave. He says, "There is something wrong with Mary. She just said that she has to check with herself to see if it is okay for her to take a break." As John is saying that to Dave, Dave turns and points to me and says, "There are two today." It was pretty funny. Years later Toni had the opportunity to work with John and they became friends.

My manager had no idea that I was fragile. I tried for years not to let that side of me out. Since I found God, though, I was much more sensitive and nervous at times. I was feeling my feelings . . . . This was still new for me. I had been a master at pushing down my feelings; I also used anger as a defense. Neither my boss nor I had any idea at this time that my past abuse issues were being triggered. I was an assistant GM manager; I was amazed that I had done as well as I did. I was moving up in management.

Liverpool Store, November 1987-May 1989

I had been employed in Liverpool for almost 18 months when the assistant GM manager position opened up in Dewitt. It would be a promotion if I got the job because it was for full time, 40 hours, with a $3 an hour raise. The promotion was because the Dewitt store was larger—a superstore—and the sales were therefore much higher.

I will always be grateful to my manager because she trained me and made sure that I was ready for the interview. I was putting up the merchandise/stock and had a lot of work to do when she said, "Mary, come here." I immediately followed her. At first I thought I was in trouble, but then I realized she was going to prepare me for the interview.

She pulled out the paperwork and showed me a T-sheet

and a lot of other things. She even said that I was a quick learn-er!! She had no idea what that meant to me.

The GM manager in the Dewitt store was Bill, and he and I spoke often. He lived in Liverpool and would stop in the store, and we had the opportunity to get to know each other. He shared his faith in God with me and how important that was to him. I also shared with him my faith. He was a great guy and I would have loved to work for him. Therefore, not only would this position be a significant promotion, I would also get to work with Bill.

I interviewed at the Dewitt store with Bill the GM manag-er, and the store manager, Gary. I told Bill that if I didn't get the job to please call me at home because I didn't want to be upset at work.

I waited and he never called . . . . I knew that was the signal that I didn't get the job, but I wanted only God's will anyway.

I got home and the phone rang. It was Bill.

"Mary?"

"Yeah."

"I hate to make these kinds of phone calls."

I tried not to let him know that my heart just sank into my stomach in disappointment.

"Yeah . . . ."

"But Mary, you'll start in two weeks."

"What?!!"

He burst out laughing.

"What are you saying?"

"You got the job!!! I prayed to God that there would be clear direction. I didn't want a close decision with this job, because I didn't want anyone to say that I chose you because we are both Christians and friends. Even Gary said that you were the best candidate for the position."

It was May 1989, and I prayed that I would have at least one year with Bill. He was an excellent teacher.

1989-May 1990 at the Dewitt Store

At the retail store, I was the Assistant General Merchandise Manager working with Bill, who was a great boss. He provided a safe environment for development. He was approachable and open. He told me to make decisions, and then **if** I made a mistake and he confronted me, to tell him that I did what **I thought** was best. He preferred that I learn from my mistakes instead of depending on him.

During this time there was another manager who worked in another department. One day when Bill was off and I was working the second shift, I entered the store around noontime. I walked into my office and had not even taken my coat off when this other department manager came in.

He was angry and said, "WHO TOLD YOU TO PUT THOSE ITEMS IN MY DEPARTMENT?!!!!"

I felt pain in my stomach, a scary feeling kind of like butterflies, and I could feel the old rage inside of me. I immediately took a deep breath, knowing that I needed God right NOW. I knew that a soft answer turns away wrath (Proverbs 15: 1). This was a test. As soon as I identified this interaction as a test, I said in my head, "This is a test. This is just a test. I had a choice: to yield to the Spirit or to the flesh, the brat Mary. I prayed and yielded to the Spirit.

I said very calmly, "First, I just walked in the door; second, I have never allowed anyone in my department to put products in your department without asking you first; and third, I do not appreciate you talking to me in that tone."

The manager just looked at me, and then in an appropriate tone of voice said that my merchandiser had put some items in his department, and the district manager did a walk through and said that the product looked sloppy.

I apologized to the manager and told him that I would have the product removed and would explain to the individual the protocol for merchandising.

I mention this to point out how God was teaching me. He was counseling me, teaching me effective adaptive coping skills. I wasn't aware then that I was learning new coping skills; it wasn't until much later that I saw what God was doing.

I still was attending the Bible-based church, and I often heard people say, "There is no love there." I didn't understand what they meant. No love??? Well, I thought that there was love there. It was familiar to me. As I look back, I now understand how I fell into this legalistic church (Legalistic means that one is under the law and rules, and if you do not conform to man's rules in dress or church attendance you are not a good Christian—less than one who follows the rules.) First, I never measured up at home; my mom and dad were not proud of me. I could never do anything right. I was always in trouble. Second, the pastor often preached a message of fear. Consequently, I felt comfortable; living in fear most of my life I never knew unconditional love and safety. Attending that church for 16 years therefore felt normal. In the early years he preached truth; nonetheless he was unapproachable. I was able to call him that first year when Toni's baby died, but that was a moot point since when I did call I didn't receive any comfort. Eventually his phone number was unlisted.

The church had those who were accepted and those who were not. As always I continued to feel like a second-class citizen. As time went on I began to see some of the contradictions with the word of God. The pastor taught a doctrine of works, and although they believed in the Gospel, the good news of John 3:16, they taught and practiced in a manner that put each individual under a law of dos and don'ts.

While working at the retail store I felt accepted. I was an assistant manager and beginning to feel okay about myself. I wore pants at work and finally became comfortable with that fact. I so often lived under condemnation because I did not always wear a dress or skirt. As members of this church, women were expected to wear dresses or skirts ALL of the time.

It was January 1990 and my mom had the flu. I was on the phone with my brother Harry, who was down visiting Mom, and he said she was pretty sick. On Sunday, Toni called me around 10 PM and asked if Chuck could stop at Mom's house to check on her, because she was **not answering the phone.** Chuck was getting ready to leave for work at Dairylea on Burnet Ave., walking distance from Mom's house. He said he was happy to check on her. I began to remove the house key from my key chain and the phone rang again.

"Mary, it's me." (It was Toni.)

"Yeah."

"I just spoke with Mom."

"Okay."

"She said that she didn't answer 'because she was asleep."

"So . . . she's okay?"

"Yeah, she said that she thinks she has the flu and is really tired."

So I put the key back on my key chain.

I worked on Monday and didn't give any thought to Mom; I was very busy.

Tuesday I went to work; my sister-in-law Tina worked with me at this retail store. In fact, she worked for me as one of the associates in the GM department. While at lunch we were talking about how the flu was going around. I said that my mom was sick but I was sure that she would be fine since she was a fighter. Bill my boss was there, too. I said, "I'll stop by and check on her before I go to my Sunday school meeting tonight."

Chuck had worked the overnight shift. Normally he would get some rest, but he wanted to get on the day schedule so after work he stayed up; he didn't go to sleep that day. He knew that I had a meeting, around 7 PM so he stayed up until I went to the meeting and then he went to bed. The boys were 15, 13, and 11 years old, so of course they were fine being in the house while he slept.

It was January 23, 1990 I called my mom, but she didn't answer the phone. I thought, *What will I do if she's dead? Well, I'll let Gary take my car to the meeting.* I felt strangely calm and had a knowing feeling.

I called Gary so we could ride to the church together. I asked him if he minded if I stopped at my mom's, explaining that she was not answering her phone. (*Gary had come with me in the past to stop at my mom's before our Sunday school meetings; therefore the request was not unusual.*) He had his two children, Craig and Stacy, with him.

We drove to my mom's house, and during the 20-minute ride I began to think, *This makes no sense. She's not dead, just sleeping or refusing to answer the phone.* So I pushed the thought out of my head. **But deep down I knew she was dead.**

I knew she was gone. The moment I saw the mail in the mailbox, I knew ... she had not checked her mail today, or the day before. As I walked down the driveway towards the back door, I knew. She always got her mail. Her paranoid mind would not allow her to neglect it, not for one day ....

Gary sensed my concern and walked with me to the back door. Craig and Stacy, Gary's two children, waited in the car. I entered through the back porch and then through the swinging door. To my right I saw her leg. I then said out loud to Gary what I already knew in my heart: "She's dead." Gary went over to her to feel for a pulse in her neck. Her eyes were open and very black.

I felt bad because she would always say, "No one cares about me! I'll be left alone dead for days before anyone realizes that I'm dead!"

I heard those words in my head and the pain of guilt emerged. I thought to myself, *I am not going to feel that awful guilt.* I chose not to believe that lie. I knew that **I loved my mom and had forgiven her.** I put myself in harm's way with her time and time again because **I never wanted her to feel**

unloved, as I had felt for a good part of my life.

It was sad that she always looked at what she didn't have. She was not a grateful individual, and that is why she was tormented until her death: she focused on disappointments. Her main problem was her negative thinking. She had identical twins whom she didn't seem to want. I could not name all of her errors in thinking, but it saddens me that she never sought out help.

I called my husband and told him she was dead. I gave my car keys to Gary to drive to the meeting and then home. My husband immediately got in the car and told the boys that he had to go down to Grandma's house. He didn't tell them what I had said, but they knew something was wrong. Their father had been awake for 23 hours and just left after one phone call. Chuck told me to call 911.

I called and told them that I had found my mom dead. I heard the sirens, and the panic on Elm Street erupted. Next door to my mom's house is my grandma's house. In minutes the news spread to the family. My cousin Toni was at the Sunday school meeting; her mother, my Aunt Fay, had just died at home (at Grandma's house next door in September). I felt awful that Toni found out at the meeting. She came over to my mom's as soon as she could get there. Harry went and got Toni in Oneida where she was working second shift as a video manager. She was very upset and felt so guilty, because the EMT said Mom must have died shortly after she talked to Toni on Sunday night.

I did cry when Mom died. It was weird: I worried at first about her soul. Did she make it to heaven? She was Catholic; although she did not practice her religion she believed. I came to the conclusion that it's not for me to know. As far as I knew, she had not accepted Christ as her Lord and Savior, but who knows how her last moments were? I decided to trust God. He makes no mistakes and I hope that she made it to heaven. She thought that she suffered enough on this earth; therefore, she had paid her dues so she would be in heaven. Well, she was not perfect, so all the suffering she had would not buy her a place in heaven. **Only a perfect sacrifice will be accepted as an atonement or payment for sin. Jesus made the only perfect sacrifice, completed once and for all on Calvary's cross. All we have to do is accept Him as our Savior; it is by his shed blood that we will enter heaven. Through His suffering we receive eternal life, not by works of righteousness lest anyone should boast (Ephesians 2: 9).**

It was strange after she died because I often expected her to call me, and when I didn't talk to her I felt the need to call her. The phone would ring and it wasn't her, but if I didn't call her at least four times a week I would be in trouble with her. Toni had a hard time because she was the one who talked to her the most. Also, she felt guilty. Bill, Toni's husband, said this was how it was meant to be.

After Mom died my life was less stressful, which may sound strange to some. Although I missed her at times, I no longer had to worry about her outrage or her disapproval of me, and I didn't have to listen to her constant belittling. I felt a sense of relief when the holidays came. No more "who is in the doghouse today?"

While I was working at the store there was a customer who was devastated that her mom had died. I listened to her, and when I told her that my mom had recently died, this woman was so compassionate that I couldn't understand her sympathy. I began to realize that most people have an extremely tough time when they lose a parent.

As I began to see how different I was, I identified more with the loss of my father-in-law, Mr. Alfonso Sorrendino. I really loved him; he was a real father figure to me. I could talk to him; he understood, and he always calmed me down if I was upset about something. I had a more difficult time getting over the loss of him than over my own parents.

In May 1990 a position opened for General Merchandise manager in another local store. This would be the next step in my grocery store career. I was presently an assistant GM manager in a large volume store, and now a manager in a small store was the way to go. I had worked with Bill for one year just as I had prayed for. I interviewed, and of the three candidates I was chosen for the job.

I worked at that store for almost nine years. This was a time of growth; I still had much insecurity and was amazed that I was now a department head. In the beginning I was indeed promoted to incompetence and did not understand as much as I thought I did. My boss at the time was very bright and had little tolerance for ignorance. The sad thing was that he had no idea that I was damaged goods, just as my other boss in Liverpool did not understand. The fact is that I needed someone like Bill to supervise me. All I needed was direction with care. When my boss was upset with me he was abusive. He was stressed out, so I received his wrath. He **did** have reason to be upset with me. In the early years I would mess up on inventory due to lack of training. Nonetheless, his frustration would exacerbate my anxiety and I couldn't think straight.

I remember having yearly reviews at which he knew that I was going to cry throughout the session. It was embarrassing for me. He had no idea, and neither did I, that he was triggering my past (post-traumatic stress disorder (PTSD). At this time I didn't know what was wrong with me. As the years went by and I became more competent, with his help I did learn. Unfortunately, he was not the best teacher for someone with my past abuse history.

Eventually he said, "I know that you're **not** an ignoramus because there is no way you could do this job, but you should learn how to write, because if someone else saw your writing they would think that you're an ignoramus."

I'm defective, less than stupid, a loser. I believe that if he had any idea that he was causing me psychological damage, he wouldn't have managed me that way. If I had gone to counseling I would have been able to handle it by telling him what I was experiencing. Or, if I couldn't communicate it, at least I would have known what was going on with me. That information could have empowered me.

Although I perceived this boss was tough on me, he was a wonderful and extremely supportive boss when my son Jason had surgery on his legs. Jason had surgery during the winter break of February 1993. He was in the hospital for 10 days, and he turned 15 while he was there.

During this hospital stay, Jason had two different roommates. One young boy was named David, and his mother's name was Mary. This young boy attended the Church of the Resurrection, and his pastor came up to visit him. The other young boy's name was Tony; he attended Abundant Life, another Christian church in Syracuse. While he was there his youth pastor visited him. I was asked, "When will your pastor be coming up?" I said that he would not be coming. Then they asked, "When will the youth pastor come up and visit?" I said, "We don't have a youth pastor."

I told them that the principal of the school gave me his home number and asked me to call him with updates. I was not to give the phone number out, but I knew that the principal really cared about my son's well being. Jason went through a lot: he had his legs turned and it was a long recuperation period. He was laid up for a few months. After his bones healed he had to have extensive physical therapy, so we returned to Joanne Barry in Liverpool.

I could not begin to mention everything that I experienced while working those nine years. I had health issues and four surgeries, one of which was major.

I also met one of my closest friends at that store, Beth. She is an amazing lady. She worked as the price accuracy coordinator (PAC). Beth provided a loving and nurturing place of safety for me. It was as though I had known her all my life. We were instant friends.

When I first started out I was amazed at how other managers could look at a wall in the back room and estimate how much inventory was there. I eventually was able to do that as well. A lot of individuals at the store were positive influences in my life and I thank God for them. I loved the business, and I loved to learn about market shares and who was holding the market in different areas

During this time in my life I was facing my fears and overcoming them. My oldest son Chuck had seen my struggle at work and how nervous I would get. One night at the dinner table I announced to my children (my husband and I had already discussed it) that I was going to step down from my position as manager. Chuckie said, "Mom, I never thought of you as a quitter." Those words resonated with me; he was right! I am not a quitter and I decided to stick it out. I faced the fear and was able to advocate for myself. I thank my God for ministering to me during this time, because He enabled me to stand on the truth: "I can do all things through Christ who strengthens me." He gave me the job; he opened the door. He was in control.

In May 1997 I began to have terrible pain in my left shoulder, radiating up my neck and all the way down my arm. My son Jason was working with me at the store; he was just 18 and attending community college at the time. He often had to drive me home; due to the level of pain I was unable to drive.

Then it was realized surgery was the only option. I was in an awful lot of pain. My son Chuckie took me to the one-day surgery center. After Dr. Hootnick finished he came out and told Chuckie that the damage was more than he could fix arthroscopically, and he would have to have me be admitted for a shoulder stabilization procedure. The doctor explained there was no cushion to hold the shoulder and it was sliding part way out of its socket. I had surgery a week later.

This shoulder injury was due to overuse, specifically over-head lifting, and I did not play sports and was not a weight-lifter; therefore this was clearly a compensation injury result-ing from working in retail.

After the surgery in August 1997, I was out of work for 6-8 weeks. When I returned in mid September, I had to be very careful.

* * * *

The End of That Bible Church

In June of 1997 my sister Toni decided to leave the church that we had been at for years. Her two sons Billy (13) and Pauly (11) were playing sports with the community leagues and often made the all-stars. Toni's husband Bill grew up in Minoa and he also played little league when he was a boy. He helped out by coaching the boys' team one year and, eventually Bill became an umpire.

Toni's reason for leaving the church was because she was not getting fed anymore. Also, she felt they would make nega-tive statements about other Christian churches, and she want-ed her boys to learn to respect other people's beliefs and love all people. Toni had had a relationship with God throughout her life. This church had a private school and all of our chil-dren went there: Tami Billy, and Pauly, and my boys Chuckie, Jason, and Eric. Tami, Chuckie, and Jason had already gradu-ated. We thought that the school was in their best interest, which is why we sacrificed to pay the tuition. Nonetheless Toni felt the Lord leading her to a different church. So in June of 1997 Toni left and began to attend the Church of the Resurrection.

My son Eric began school in September and a lot of strange things were going on. Some 16-year-old boys were kicked out of their homes because they were acting out. Eric was very upset at some of the parents, because he thought that they were too harsh and unloving; it appeared to him that in an effort to force their children to attend that school they would kick them out of the house. Anyway, Eric decided to leave and then attended Cicero High School. He also began to attend church with Aunt Toni.

At this time my husband began to attend the Church of the Resurrection in an effort to be a responsible parent. He thought that we needed to check out the church. Chuck went one time and was sold; he said that he would never return to the other church. I began attending both churches.

* * * *

In early February 1998, the chain of retail stores was going through an acquisition, actually switching from one greeting card vendor to another one. This procedure required supervision from a GM manager, but the Oswego GM manager was on vacation that week. My own store was very small, and I was asked to help out at the much larger Oswego store because I was a trained manager. A LOT of inventory dollars would be lost if the step-by-step process was not executed according to protocol.

The Friday prior to going to the other store, I was coming down the spiral steps from the store manager's office and I slipped! I grabbed hold of the handrail with my left hand and I could feel my arm pull out of socket. It was just six months since my surgery and the pain was intense.

I thought *OH NO, I did something!!!* The front-end supervisor was there and saw me fall. She said, "You really messed up that arm now." She could see the pain in my face.

I went to see Dr. Hootnick because of the pain. He wanted to keep me out of work, but I wouldn't take off time because I had the Oswego store to run next week and there was

NO ONE else who could do it! I begged my doctor, "Please, I'll keep it in the sling."

He reluctantly let me go to work on limited duty. I was able to work at the Oswego store and I tried hard to follow my surgeon's restrictions, but it was impossible for me not to move the arm at all. I was suffering, and each day the pain would increase throughout the day.

I went to work on Thursday and made sure that everything for the greeting card section was done, paperwork included. I knew that I must have looked awful. My shoulder and arm were hurting so excruciatingly that I knew Dr. Hootnick was not going to be happy. I walked into his office that day around 4:00 and didn't say a word. He said, "That's it, I'm taking you out of work!!!"

I returned to Joanne Barry in Liverpool for physical therapy. Eventually, by March, I returned to work.

I always had pain, but I was growing accustomed to it. At home, washing dishes was extremely painful. We didn't have a dishwasher, so I had the repetitive action of putting the dishes with my left arm into the drain board to my left.

In June 1998 I was in the back room at work lifting a large box. It was not heavy, just very cumbersome, but as I lifted the box over my head my left shoulder gave out and the box dropped on my face! The pain was intense! I was so frustrated!!! After that, my shoulder pain returned with a vengeance. My Uncle Sandy drove for the company back then and he would help me, as did many of my co-workers. I pressed on, hoping that I would get better.

* * * *

I was very active at the store, and I was the one who would plan the Christmas parties and the picnics; I also helped with fundraisers. I believed that we needed to reach the lost and show the love of God. I would have Christmas parties with alcohol, though I did not drink and I made sure that everyone got home safely. At my church I was looked down on because I attended these functions. I did it anyway. I was so used to being condemned that I became numb to it and did what I thought was best. I was so tired of the judgmental attitudes of some of the individuals at the church that I ignored them. I must stress that there are and have always been some wonderful Christian people attending that church who love others, and are not judgmental. They love God and they encouraged me when I was there. When Toni left, everyone was saying that I was going to leave. I said, "I will only leave if God tells me to."

On a Thursday night at Resurrection, the Rev. Iris Godfrey taught about the holidays. She said, "As the holidays draw near you will be attending work functions and family functions. Go and glow!!" I was surprised that she was preaching what I believed and lived!!

In December of 1997 I was praying to God and I asked Him to please show me the way. I asked that he would show me just as he did when I was first saved! God spoke to my heart and said, "Do you still give your boys a bottle?" I knew then that God was directing me to his Word. I read in Scripture that the husband is the head and that I should follow him. I also knew that the teaching from the pulpit at Resurrection brought life to my spirit. I was so thirsty for good teaching that did not condemn me or other churches. In December I left that church; after 16 years of attendance I was FREE and felt as if I had been born again, again.

During this summer my nephews Billy and Pauly, now 14 and 12, were getting big. They were getting more interested in bicycling. Chuck and I biked a lot, and our boys always biked with us.

I was off on Mondays, so one Monday Billy and I took a ride together from Kirkville to Minoa. We went down to the canal and rode to Minoa, where we got off the trail and went down the main street. We stopped at Billy's grandmother's house and visited with Mr. and Mrs. Wood. Mr. Wood thought that I was Toni for just a minute. We had a great time, and I was already planning our next ride.

We talked about the difference between disability and compensation. Although my left arm still hurt, if I was not lifting it was okay to ride.

I was still working at the same store and we were redoing our house. We got all new windows and siding. We knocked out the wall that went into the garage and had the living room turned into a 27-foot room. We also were getting a dining room.

Life was good. Billy and Pauly loved the new church, and Billy was very involved with the youth group. Attending a convention, he was amazed at how many Christian kids were in Syracuse. While attending the other church, he thought that we were the only ones. Billy said to his mom, "Maybe Resurrection is not for everyone, but it is for us." He loved it there.

On Wednesday, July 8, Toni, Billy, and Pauly came to my house to see the progress. I asked Toni to help me with shelf lining in the new breakfast bar area. She was in a hurry as always, but we had a nice visit. Billy asked me where my floor in the dining room would end. I showed him. The Pergo was delivered and would be installed sometime during the week. He was very interested in the remodeling project. While Toni and I worked on lining the shelves Billy and Pauly went out front with their Uncle Chuck and played catch with the Frisbee.

When Billy left he gave me a hug in my driveway, and I asked him if he liked the new shutters.

"Yeah, I like them."

"Uncle Chuck picked them out."

"Nice . . . ." He gave me a hug and a kiss and said, "I love you."

On Thursday I went to work. It was a beautiful day out, sunny and warm.

Billy and Pauly were at the house of their grandma, Mrs.

Wood, in Minoa. Billy was talking with her about next week and he told her, "Mom and Dad are going to be on vacation and we're supposed to go to Canada and see the Toronto Blue Jays play, but I think that something is going to come up and we aren't going to make the trip."

Mrs. Wood said, "Don't worry; you know that your parents will work it out. They always do."

Most of the morning Billy was planning to meet up with his friend Mitch.

Around 1:00 PM in the afternoon Billy left his grandmother's with permission to meet Mitch.

He crossed the street so he would be on the right side, as I had taught him to ride with the traffic.

I came home from work and there was a message from my brother-in-law Bill's sister Sharon, which I thought was odd. I called her back and she was apprehensive.

I said, "What's going on?"

"Well . . . are you alone?"

"Yes. What?"

"Could you please come to my mom's house?"

"What's going on?"

"I'd rather not say on the phone."

I continued to press her, and then my sister Toni got on the phone and said that I should come to the house.

"What's going on?!!!"

"Mary, Billy got hit riding his bike."

My heart dropped to the pit of my stomach. "What hospital?"

Toni said, "He's dead."

Oh my God, **I could not breath.** I was going to throw up. My brain could not wrap around this. *I can't go to the hospital and say good-bye.*

I had never had to experience the pain of such a loss, and I pray that I never will again.

My brother-in-law Bill drove over to get me. They all knew

how close I was to Billy and that I should not be alone. I talked to Billy daily. When I called Toni he would get on the phone and talk with me. His mom, joking with him, would say, "She called for me!"

Bill arrived and found me in the dining room on the cement floor. I was an emotional wreck. He peeled me off of the floor and held me; I was sobbing and not taking full breaths. He said, "It's okay, let it out."

The blood-curdling scream was the sound of excruciating pain. I collapsed in Bill's arms. Cathie Bosma, Gary's wife, heard the cry from across the street and she ran to my house to see if I was okay, but she KNEW that I wasn't.

Billy had a huge funeral—three blocks of cars. He touched so many lives from our former church and the Church of the Resurrection, his school, his little league, and even from the grocery store. Our family and the Prince family all came to pay respects. Farones, the funeral home, had to have the police direct traffic.

The next few weeks were hell. I thought, and God is my witness, that I should find some weed and get high. THE THOUGHT CROSSED MY MIND BECAUSE I COULD NOT BEAR THE PAIN!!! In the mornings when my alarm went off I could barely open my eyes. *HOW AM I GOING TO BREATHE IN THIS WORLD WITHOUT BILLY?!* I would wonder. *HOW CAN I LIVE WITHOUT HIM IN MY LIFE?* I could not imagine what Toni, Bill, Tami, and Pauly were suffering when I couldn't take the pain.

I began to focus on Pauly; someone had to. Toni and Bill were in the depths of despair, and he was so alone. Tami was living in Buffalo, because that was where her fiancé David was working. Therefore she was not able to be local, although she was a phone call away if Pauly needed her. I began to watch Pokemon every morning before work, so when I called Pauly in the evening we would have something to talk about.

The pain was so unbearable at times that I thought I would die from a broken heart. I felt like God reached into my chest and pulled out my heart. Then He ran it through a shredder and put it back into me all bloody.

I questioned God: how could He have allowed this to happen?!!! I was so very angry and confused. One day when I was ready to give up on God and return to my drugs, I made a choice to call my pastor, Tim Adour.

I told him of my pain and how I was questioning God. It was as though I wouldn't let God comfort me. He would try and I would fight against Him. Pastor said that God has big shoulders and He knows my pain. He wants to help me and He is with me; despite the anger and rage that I am experiencing, I can know that He loves me. Back at the other church, my sons Chuckie and Jason were still attending. If they left that church they would lose their whole support system. As a rule at this former church, if people leave the church it is believed that they have rebelled and have left the Lord, and no one is to keep contact with them. The pastor stated from the pulpit that he knew a lot of individuals were supportive to the Wood family during this time; however, they should not continue with contact. The fact is that there was a tremendous outpouring of love and support from many of the members of that church. There was one family that took Paul with them on family vacations and never turned their back on him despite the direction from the pulpit. My sister Toni is forever grateful to that family and others who reached out. Still, my boys Chuckie and Jason continued at the church.

In one service the pastor said that a young lady who attended the church had thought that God was sending her elsewhere, and now her son is dead. After that service he spoke directly to my brother John and said, "If your sister hadn't left this church, her son would be alive today." Everyone knew that he was referring to Toni. It was then that my boys left the church and came to the Resurrection. Pastor Tim told me, "If that is his God, it's not the same one that we serve." He said that was a lie from the pit of hell and I needed to stand on the truth.

Toni worked at Beacon Federal; the president of the bank, Ross Prossner, was amazing. He addressed this situation and said that Toni would need the support of her fellow employees to get through this tragedy. So he brought Toni to Hope for the Bereaved a local agency that helps those in need of supports. After Toni was introduced to this agency Toni and I went together. Theresa Shonock began this outreach to parents who have lost their children. Toni also is grateful to God for putting the supportive individuals in her life at Beacon, and others such as Barb Giocondo, and Carl and Diane Putzer (*there are too many to name*) when she needed them the most. I must say that if not for the support and our faith in God, we could not have made it through the pain.

I learned that grief is so HIGH that you can't go over it, so LOW you can't go under it, so WIDE you can't go around it. The only way is to go through the pain of grief, and then to come to acceptance. That work is exhausting.

This may not sound like much to anyone reading this, but I know that if I had returned to drugs then, this book would have never been written. To deal completely with this topic of grief would take another book.

I returned to work and was a mess. My shoulder was getting worse, and by late August I was again out of work. After extensive therapy it was determined that the shoulder was shot.

The plan was to return to work as an office clerk. This felt weird. First, I did not like working with money. Second, I was used to being in charge. I began a six-week training program for office clerk. It turned out to be training for office supervisor, and I was overwhelmed. I began to train in January 1999, and by February I was out of a job. I had a shortage, and it was determined that I was not going to work out as an office clerk and I was terminated.

I went to see my doctor, and he said maybe re-training was the answer. I, of course, had a compensation case and was talking with my attorney, and he said the same thing. "Maybe you can't work in retail, but you could go back to school and train for a new career."

✳ ✳ ✳ ✳

Things were tough for a long time after Billy died. I was blessed at the Church of the Resurrection, where the people were supportive and caring. I met this guy Kevin Rivers who worked for Frito-Lay. Since I had worked in the grocery business, we learned that we knew a lot of the same people. We were in a discipleship class together while his wife Laurie was working with the youth group. On Thursday nights at church, Kevin would sit with Toni and me.

One Thursday night Kevin was so excited; he had some great news but I was sworn to secrecy. Kevin said, "Laurie is pregnant!" They were so happy. Laurie was a Spanish teacher in the East Syracuse school district.

Now in January 1999 they had a beautiful baby girl named Audrey Elizabeth Rivers. When they would come to church on Thursdays, Kevin would have his daughter and he would let me hold her. I thought that was great. Eventually he asked me if I would be interested in babysitting for his daughter when Laurie returned to school in the spring. I said, "I'll have to pray about it and talk to my husband." Kevin knew that I was out of a job due to my arm and was always being cautious with it. Even when I would hold Audrey I would have my left arm supported because it didn't take much to aggravate it.

I decided to watch her, and Kevin was blessed. He and Laurie had prayed, asking God who should watch Audrey, because she had stopped breathing once and they were very afraid to leave her.

I began to babysit in the spring of 1999. It was not long before I fell in love with that little girl. Soon her mom was calling me Aunt Mary. Audrey was a quick learner and began to talk very early. By the time she was seven months old she would answer when I asked her: "What does the lamb say?" Audrey would say, "Baaa."

I spent a lot of time with her, and she grew so attached to me that during church she would cry to come to me. One time when she was just learning to walk she tried to follow me out the door. She would run into my arms like in the movies. She is a very special person in my life, and definitely a gift from God to me. I became a part of that family. In March of 2001, Ian Matthew Rivers was born, and what a blessing I have being a part of that family.

PART VI
The Healing
and Ministry

In 1982, God had showed me that I would be a counselor or a psychologist someday, and of course this came back to mind. I talked with Chuck and he said, "Well, you can start out at OCC [Onondaga Community College]." I looked at the catalog and read about the Human Services curriculum. In that explanation it mentioned that this curriculum would position an individual for a career in alcohol and substance abuse counseling. I had not known that there was a special field for that type of counseling. At this time, OCC did not have the CASAC (Credentialed Alcoholism and Substance Abuse Counselor) coursework within the curriculum. The choices were Human Services and social work or Human Services and Early Childhood Education. After talking with some people at the college, I decided to enter the Human Service / Social Work program.

I went to OCC and took the entrance exam. I failed math . . . and writing. My math was so below level that I had to start by taking non-credit courses. I started out at the math lab that summer. My packets that I had to work on were subtraction, division, and multiplying. I also had to work on decimals.

I began to work very hard until I was able to enter my first year of college taking algebra. Now, algebra is a non-credit math course, yet I struggled. Despite the extra help I was not able to understand. My three sons are math whizzes. Chuckie had taken **calculus.** Meanwhile, their mother could not do times tables.

I began classes in the fall of 1999. I read the requirements, which said that you must carry a C in all courses in your major. My heart began to race; I could not imagine that I could get C's. Surely not in all of my course work! The anxiety increased.

During the summer I also took a non-credit English class because my writing was very low, and to matriculate one must be at college level to take the first Human Services class. Thank God I learned that and was allowed to take that non-credit course. I passed it and was then matriculated into my major.

I knew that I was in God's will, but I could not see how this was going to work out at all. I took Psychology 101 with Professor DiPerna, who was a great instructor. During class I was able to answer the questions. After studying my head off for the first exam, though, I barely passed it. I was shook up, almost in tears! The panic began to grip me and I **knew** that it was hopeless. *I'm stupid and I'm not able to learn. Whatever made me think I could do this????*

The professor and one of my classmates saw the pain in my face. Professor DiPerna called me over and asked, "Did you get nervous taking this exam?"

"Yes, I studied so hard and still I couldn't do it. Everyone was getting up and they were done and I was still there working."

"Mary, you're studying too much. I only want you to cover what's on this syllabus, okay?"

"Okay."

"Now, I want you to make flash cards. And know that I am NOT timing you. If you don't get done in time, you can finish it in my office on my couch."

"Okay."

My classmate, Erik, came over and he saw how upset I was. He had gotten an A and said that he would love to start a study group. So Erik, another nontraditional student, and I began our study group.

Once the pressure was off it was amazing: I began to get A's in Psychology. My Human Services course was going great. On one test I was the only one who got an A. I ended up being exempt from the final due to the straight A's. Unbelievable!

Nonetheless, math still was hard for me. I was struggling

as always. I would go for extra help, and I would get it and then lose it. I was also struggling in English.

I was still watching Audrey but not full time due to school. Laurie would help me with the math, and she would proof-read my papers.

First Internship at the Willows

During the fall of 1999 I began to explore possible intern-ships. I was interested in the drug and alcohol field, so I went to Syracuse Behavioral Healthcare, to the Willows in-patient facility, which was located on Onondaga Hill near the Van Dyne Nursing Home. The building was nostalgic and very old. It had been used as a sanitarium back at the turn of the century.

My first meeting was with the clinical team leader, Bob Walsh. He asked me why I was interested in this field, and I said that I used to use drugs and believed that there were a lot of individuals who had rough upbringings and needed help. I wanted to help them. He understood and asked me to read a book by James Garbarino called *The Lost Boys*. I told him that I owned the book and had already read it. At that time I thought that one day I might work with teens, like at Teen Challenge. Bob said that a lot of their clients were like teens because they began to use in their teens and stunted their psy-chological growth.

I loved working there, learning something every day. I worked with Collette, and I loved the way she would express unconditional positive regard. She really cared. I began to work in admissions, and eventually I would get to do the admissions by myself.

I had some concerns . . . . I have a very strong sense of smell. While working in the retail store, I had a few experiences where a customer who was probably homeless came into the store and the smell was just too much! Well, one day I had an opportunity to work with this man who had arrived from the justice center. He apologized to me for his body odor, stating that he had not showered since he was incarcerated. It was very warm in the interview room, and I suggested that he take his coat off.

"Oh no, I can't. The smell is bad!"

I said, "Well, let me tell you, I have a very sensitive nose and I don't smell anything, so it's okay."

He took his coat off. We were in that room for an hour, and when we finished I walked him down the hall to the nurse's office.

When I went through the paperwork, I realized I had forgotten to give the nurse something. I walked back down the hall and there was this nasty smell. The smell was nauseating; I could barely walk into the nurse's office.

I said, "What is that?!"

The nurse looked at me in shock! "Mary, it was that client. You were with him for an hour!"

As I left that office I KNEW that God had protected me, knowing that I was not able to show the love of God to that man if I smelled him. I knew I was in the right field.

I met James Holloman, a strong African-American man about five years older than me who stood six feet four inches tall. I was allowed to sit in on his men's group; it was very powerful. I thought that he was an amazing counselor.

I then met Lloyd Mills. He was working in the office where the head of admissions worked. After we finished admitting a client we had to write a narrative clinical summary. One big weakness for me is writing, and I of course asked Lloyd for help. He was about 12 years my senior and a solid, very strong man. His hands were huge. Originally from Kansas, he stood about six feet two inches. My first impression was that he was probably one of the smartest men I had ever met. He began to dictate the clinical summary: "Client's use exacerbated his existing legal ramifications." I had NEVER heard anyone talk in clinical terms and I was impressed!!!

I also met Phyllis Perrone but did not work closely with her. I shadowed her one day.

At the end of the first semester I ended up with a 3.50 GPA. I made the dean's list! I did fail math, but it was a non-credit course so it didn't affect my GPA. I also got a C in English.

I was devastated over the math. Laurie Rivers wrote me a card from Audrey that said, "The only math that matters is **Aunt Mary + Audrey = LOVE.**" The encouragement from Laurie was indescribable. Here was this incredible woman, an intelligent overachiever, who made me feel accepted even though I felt like a failure. How she saw the potential in me is beyond my comprehension, but she saw something other than the stupid, low-class individual that I felt inside.

What I learned later was that my shame-based sense of self was raising its ugly head again. I forgot that I am a child of God; instead I felt like a loser.

During January 2000, I took a 10-day class as a second try to learn the math that I had failed. I took the final test in two parts, which slowed it down for me. I ended up getting an 82 and an 89 on the final!!!!! I was amazed that I passed and was ready to take a college-level math course.

The next semester I got a great English teacher, Dr. Place. He was going to push me until I handed in a paper that earned an A!!! I also had Emily Miller, an excellent teacher who taught communications class. That was one of the best classes I ever took.

Then there was my awesome mentor, Barbra McLean. She taught me so much and was a great role model. I had never been to counseling in my life, and she was the first person who demonstrated unconditional positive regard toward me. I felt it when I went to her because I was overwhelmed. She made me feel safe; she was able to help me help myself.

* * * *

I took a class about domestic violence that was a turning point for me. My teacher showed videos of different scenarios. As I watched the abuse during class I became emotional—very emotional. I have always looked at my past and thought it was tough, but so MANY have had it much worse. Although this is true, it does NOT NEGATE THE FACT THAT I SUFFERED SERIOUS PSYCHOLOGICAL DAMAGE. I had to read a book about children being abused, and I saw myself as the victim in the chapter on sexual abuse.

I also figured out that my intense fear of being alone at night came from not being safe in my own home as a child, especially at night!

Although God did bring me through, if I had sought out counseling I could have normalized the experience and found safety sooner. Many individuals are abused and never develop PTSD, symptoms of PTSD, or anxiety disorders. **The fact is, I did.**

As I neared the end of my first year my husband said that I should go on and get my B.A. By now my GPA was 3.8, and he was impressed with my grades.

Near the close of the semester at the end of my first year, Professor Carl DiPerna asked, "Mary, are you going to continue your education?"

I said, "No, I don't think so . . . ."

"Why?"

"Well, I don't think I can do it, and I need to get a job."

"Mary, you are an **excellent candidate for a bachelor's degree.**"

I was **shocked t**hat someone would ever suggest that.

Back home my husband encouraged me to look into a university. One thing Chuck did say was that I could not spend so much time on my papers if I got into a B.A. program.

Second Internship

I knew that the time I spent in the field would count towards my Certification Alcohol and Substance Abuse Counselor (CASAC) hours as long as the organization was licensed by New York State's Office of Alcoholism and Substance Abuse Services (OASAS).

I wanted to be used by God, so I thought that I should do an internship at a Christian organization. I interviewed for an internship at the Rescue Mission's Lydia Center for women in need and I got the position, but while working there I was disappointed. I was not trusted. Certainly, as I look back I see where I had lacked some boundaries, but the supervisor would not allow me to talk to the ladies. I was devastated by the experience. My supervisor didn't know how to explain to me where I went wrong; she just stopped me from learning, saying that I had no boundaries. Today I understand why she said that; she just didn't know how to articulate what she saw. Years later, while I was working at the Willows, there were a lot of interns and new employees in the field, and I was able to articulate healthy boundaries to them so they could change.

My husband said, "Mary, Bob Walsh trusted you, and you had the opportunity to learn. Why not go back there?"

I did. I was taking 18 credit hours, interning at the Lydia Center, and volunteering at the Willows. At this time the Willows had moved. It was now at 847 James Street. My first day back at the Willows, I helped out in admissions with Joyce S. She was an excellent teacher.

A client came in from the Rescue Mission and was struggling. I listened to him and let him know that I also was in "recovery" and that God helped me. (*The fact is that God delivered me from drugs and alcohol. I was an addict; therefore, as I refer to myself as being in recovery I relate to my client. The more I've learned about the disease of addiction the clearer I see what God has done for me. I learned throughout my journey that I am no different than my clients.*) He had been listening to the preaching at the Rescue Mission and had some questions for me. I helped him with his questions. I ended up praying with the man, and he asked Jesus Christ into his heart to be his Lord and Savior.

God spoke to me and said, "It doesn't matter what it says on the outside of the building. I am IN you and will use you." It was at this point that I wanted to work full time at the Willows.

In May of 2001 I graduated from OCC with a GPA of 3.86. Of course, to some that is not that big of a deal. For me it was UNBELIEVABLE!!!! I had to **work extremely hard!** Deep down I thought I was stupid, and that is why it took me longer to get everything. The fact is that I understood a lot, but I had an awful time writing out what I knew. I even *thought* that the teachers gave me good grades because they liked me.

While at OCC, one of the adjunct instructors, Judy Murray, encouraged me to explore graduate level work. She said it would be a waste if I didn't go for an M.S. in social work.

I walked in the commencement ceremony as a nontraditional student. I had a network of friends of all ages, I felt accepted, and I was so grateful to God for this degree.

I received three scholarships: one for the Human Services, one for nontraditional students, and a merit scholarship for Oswego. I share this information so that all can see how mighty my God is! I was also a member of the honor society PHI THETA KAPPA. Unbelievable!

Oswego State

I explored different schools and my love for psychology was the deciding factor. I chose Oswego State. I was matriculated into the Human Development Psychology program. Dr. Kruse was my advisor, and she had complete confidence in me to achieve higher education. When we first met she told me that eventually I could get my Ph.D.!!! Again that an educated, intelligent individual would even think that I could consider doing that was unbelievable.

I had to get extra help with writing and statistics. Dr. Reihman was my statistics instructor. I was overwhelmed, and I had to work extra hard to get the grades that I did. Having to learn the mathematical computations made the tests dreadfully hard for me. At one point I was walking on campus and I was so overwhelmed that I asked myself, *WHAT THE HELL WERE YOU SMOKING WHEN YOU THOUGHT THAT YOU COULD DO THIS?!!!!!!*

I came home, and by this time I had to do Pearson's correlation. I was experiencing anxiety and I was plagued with fear. I made a choice that night. First I asked myself, *Did my God direct me to this curriculum?*

Yes He did.

Then I asked, *Does God know how to do this math?*

Yes He does.

So I looked at the book and prayed to God and told Him, "I'll do my best; I need you to do the rest."

I did get a B+.

I loved psychology and I really enjoyed abnormal psychology, though I had to do extra work to obtain an A. My instructor, Dr. Karen Woodford, asked if I would consider being her Teaching Assistant next semester. I was on cloud nine!! I actually get to take the course again by being in her class and helping the students. I loved to help the students and set up a study group. I was also inducted into PSI CHI, an honors society for psychology students.

I had some excellent professors; I also made friends with some wonderful, caring students. Being a nontraditional student I was comfortable being older than my classmates. Marissa LaShure was in a couple of my classes, and she and her friends truly liked me. I did not hang with them, but they obviously enjoyed my company and some would say that I was the college mom. I will forever be grateful to them for the love and acceptance that they showed to me. After two years of hard

The Healing and Ministry   *   203

work I graduated with a B.A. and ended up with a 3.60 GPA. When I graduated with my B.A. in 2003, I sat with Marissa and her friends at the commencement ceremony. I was so grateful to God for His mercy and grace.

While I was working on my B.A. my husband said, "Mary, I think you should explore graduate work. All of the want ads prefer a master's degree."

I checked out the program at Syracuse University in social work, but I just did not see me doing social work. Of course I was interested in being a clinical social worker, but I wasn't sure. I knew that **God had clearly told me** to be a therapist or a counselor.

I explored Oswego's counseling program. I found out that I could enter that program and get all of my needed course work for the Certified Alcohol and Substance Abuse Counselor CASAC and become a licensed mental health counselor (LMHC). God did so many things for me with His timing and His divine appointment. I couldn't mention all that He did to open those doors, but I was accepted at Oswego and eager to get started.

Graduate School

I graduated in May 2003 with my B.A. and immediately began my graduate work at Oswego in June. I was accepted into the school of education in the Counseling and Psychological Services department. I chose the community counseling program with the CASAC option.

This education was remarkable! I had the best professors and instructors! Dr. Jody Fiorini was my advisor, and I cannot state all of the things she did for me. Dr. Jodi Mullen was another amazing woman. These instructors really cared about and took an interest in their students. Dr. Gerald Porter mesmerized me with his knowledge and care for his students. Dr. LaBlanc taught group counseling. The staff made sure that only capable, qualified professionals would obtain a degree from Oswego.

I was a graduate assistant and received a stipend. The high school dropout who failed two grades had found herself in graduate school . . . . Now, if that's not a miracle of God I don't know what is.

During my second semester, Dr. Mullen was teaching on positive reinforcement. I was a psych major so I knew a lot of the information. Dr. Mullen was throwing chocolate kisses to the students who answered the questions correctly. Normally, I was careful not to monopolize the class, allowing other students to answer the questions. That day I couldn't hold back, because I would get CHOCOLATE!!!! I did well in class. When we had an exam on these concepts I didn't study, because Chuck and I went to Pennsylvania into the mountains the weekend prior to the test. We had a wonderful weekend. It was a gift from Laurie and Kevin.

I took the test and I froze because I hadn't studied as I have to. I got a C. Dr. Mullen said to see her; I told her that I didn't study and that was why I got a poor grade.

Dr. Mullen said, "Mary, you need to get tested."

"Well, I just didn't study and . . ."

"No, Mary, you know the information. You need to get tested."

Dr. Mullen explained that she thought I had learning disabilities. I thought she might be right.

I was upset, so I went and talked with Dr. Fiorini. She agreed with her colleague and also thought that I had a learning disability. I must admit, I did not run out and get an appointment for a psychological evaluation.

I was taking another counseling course, and I was struggling with the written assignments and had received a low grade. So I then went to meet with the instructor to inquire if I had failed to comprehend the material that was being covered. During this meeting the instructor pulled out my paper and banged the back of her hand on my paper and said, "This is **not graduate level work! Your paper needs to be flawless!!!!**" She then pulled out another classmate's paper, and said "Like Mark's!"

I was a MESS. My stomach was in knots! Fear GRABBED me, and I was coming apart at the seams! *OH MY GOD! I'VE BEEN FOUND OUT. I AM STUPID. HOW DID I MAKE IT THIS FAR?!!!!!!*

I began to be gripped by **fear.** I didn't realize that it was fear; I just felt in over my head. As afraid as I was when I was struggling in statistics class, this was 100 times worse. I could not shake this feeling. Driving to school I would break down and cry.

My husband said, "Mary, you need to talk to someone."

I got a counselor's name from my friend Sherry, Paul Honess, and I called him and left a desperate message. I was grateful that he got back to me the next day. I pulled my car off the road and he listened to me sob.

I told him how I needed to get tested for learning disabilities, and that I was a MESS. Paul is an awesome clinician, and I learned through our sessions that I was terrified that when I was tested the TRUTH would be exposed. Everyone would know that I am stupid, and once EVERYONE knew, I couldn't face them. I was shame-based, and the thought of being found out or exposed was more than I could handle. Paul explained to me that there was no way I could be in graduate school and suffer from a mental retardation diagnosis, which I feared because I thought I had heard a teacher tell my mom that my IQ was 70. The average is 100 with a standard deviation of 10; therefore an IQ of 90-110 would be average.

Paul normalized this necessary test and I made the phone call and set up the appointment.

On the big day of the first appointment, I entered the waiting room and checked in. The receptionist gave me a questionnaire to fill out. I sat there and read the questions, and I knew that I must be honest to obtain the help I needed. I couldn't believe that I was asked, "Have you ever been molested? How old were you at the time?" *WOW, this is something I just don't talk about!!!* I was feeling ashamed and dirty, but I checked "yes" and wrote "7 years old." The personal questions continued. I thought, *Man, I am MESSED UP!*

The testing took about three sessions. I really liked the doctor who tested me, and I thought that I might meet with him for counseling if he thought that I should. During the test I got extremely nervous and couldn't think. I felt like a kid again. He said, "Don't worry, I won't hit you TOO hard." I wasn't aware that I was thinking that he might hit me, but when he said it to me I realized that I wasn't fully present. I was disassociating at some level because I FELT JUST LIKE WHEN I WAS A KID!!

When all of the testing was done the truth came to light. As everyone had thought, I have learning disabilities in written communication and math. I also cannot take notes effectively. In addition to the LD, I received another diagnosis: Anxiety *not otherwise specified* (NOS). I was tested for ADD but the results were negative. My IQ was 100, average. This doctor told me he suspected that it was higher than average. He believed that my anxiety during the testing compromised the results; however, he must go with the empirical evidence, which was average.

The benefit of getting tested was that I received allowances. First, I got extra time and a separate location for my exams. Second, I was allowed to have all notes from class given to me in advance. However, I **did not use** the separate testing or the extra time, because in grad school tests were projects, and as far as the notes were concerned, most teachers gave them to everyone because they used PowerPoint.

Although I understood, I felt ashamed of the fact that I was defective.

Paul Honess is a licensed Clinical Social Worker LCSW. He helped me a lot, but he was located in Eastwood and I was attending Oswego State. Because the program I was in had some of the coursework in Watertown, I was driving **a lot.** It was impossible for me to continue counseling with Paul at the time due to the location of his office and my school.

The shame was eating at me. I felt totally rejected by that one professor, and my past demons were coming back. I was faking it, acting okay, but inside the shame was torturing me.

Finally, I went to my advisor, Dr. Jody Fiorini, and told her what that teacher had done to me. The day that professor said, "This is not graduate level work!" I began to cry and was once again overwhelmed. She called the counseling center on campus and asked to set up an appointment with Andrea.

Andrea was an incredible clinician. I felt secure with her; she allowed me to tell my story, and she knew and understood what I was saying. At times her eyes filled with tears, although she never broke down. She listened to my pain, and her empathy for me was apparent.

As we met each week, she reframed the fact that I was never Mom's or Dad's little girl. I did not have **any parent** who valued me or loved me. I knew that they **didn't love me,** but hearing someone say it out loud was powerful; she said what I could not say at the time.

She told me none of it was my fault. She had me write letters because I was not very good at role-playing. These letters were aggressive and I was angry, but writing them was a useful tool that helped me face the anger and pain and come to acceptance.

I would cry every time I met with her; I would sob just like when Billy died. That deep pain of loss and grief would be almost unbearable.

Although I had forgiven my parents, **I had never grasped the depths** of the abuse that I had forgiven. Not facing the reality fully kept me stuck. I needed to see and feel and understand that I forgave them for the psychological damage.

One thing that **I could not accept** was that it was **NOT my fault.** Deep down I blamed myself for the sexual abuse, because I did not tell on my father when I was seven years old. It was not until years later that I had to revisit that LIE. Paul Honess was the therapist who helped me process that stronghold. He is amazing, and he helped me by asking if I knew any little girls about seven years old. I thought, *Yes, my nieces Audrey, Meghan, and Noelle.* He asked me to think about them, and then he asked, "What would you say to them if they had gone through what you experienced with your dad?" I cannot even begin to tell you the rage I felt! If anyone hurt one of those little precious ones .... Paul asked if I would blame them. **"ABSOLUTELY NOT!!! THEY'RE LITTLE GIRLS!"** He then asked, "Why do you blame little Mary???" The light went on: *IT WAS NOT MY FAULT!*

I graduated from grad school on December 21, 2004, on our 30th wedding anniversary, with a 3.89 GPA. To God be the glory.

* * * *

I began to work full time at the Willows, filling in for Lloyd Mills, who was a primary counselor. He was very sick and was going into the hospital for surgery.

In March 2005 a position opened at the Evaluation Center, a crisis center that, like the Willows, is a part of Syracuse Behavioral Healthcare (SBH). I knew that God had a plan for me and I clearly saw myself at the Willows as a primary counselor. The problem was that turnover was rare. When someone got a job there, he or she did not leave. Bob Walsh was a great mentor and supervisor. He built the team and they all worked together.

Katie, a primary counselor at the Willows, was looking for another job because she was driving from Fulton to Syracuse. She was a very nice young lady, and she taught me a great deal back when I interned at the Willows. In the fall of 2004 she told me that she was looking to get another job closer to home.

There was no way at that time I could have interviewed for her job, because I had to finish my degree. Knowing that Katie was looking, I took the position at the Evaluation Center with a disclaimer. I said, "**If** a job opens up at the Willows for a full-time primary counselor, I want to interview for the job." Beth, the program director at the Evaluation Center at the time, made sure I would get the opportunity.

I loved working at the Evaluation Center because I had the opportunity to work with some colleagues who used to work at the Willows: Dawn Greene and Darlene Wagner. These two women are outstanding clinicians who care about the clients. I also met Monica, Joe, and Jeff, just wonderful people doing an amazing job helping hurting people. I worked at the Evaluation Center for six weeks.

Meanwhile, while I was working at the Evaluation Center, Katie found another job in Fulton and gave Bob her notice, opening up a position for a primary counselor at the Willows. My dream job!! Beth kept her word and made sure that I had the opportunity to interview for the job. Bob Walsh was able to give me the job, as I was already trained, had been volunteering, and had done five internships there.

It just happened that Joe Goss and I went to the Willows together. As much as I missed the team at the Evaluation Center, I knew I was where God wanted me.

When I first began I was teased about bringing the clients home with me. Now I NEVER brought a client home. However, sometimes I worked harder than the client.

All was great; I had my dream job and God was using me! I was very happy to go to work each day and see my other family: James Holloman, Lloyd Mills, Phyllis Perrone, Joe Goss, and the rest of the staff. Carol Watkins, who also attended my church, worked there as an administrative assistant. What a blessing it was to work with her; anytime I needed spiritual help I would not walk but run to her for prayer!

Lloyd Mills and I were riding to work together for a few months. Those commutes turned out to be therapy sessions for me. I was struggling with an individual who had triggered my past. I didn't know that he had triggered my past only that I was allowing this person to rent space in my head. I was sharing my frustration with Lloyd.

While talking to Lloyd he gave me the best advice, which was to read *Freedom from Bondage,* a story in the back of the *Alcoholics Anonymous* book. I read that and applied it, following the direction, and my heart changed and the stress that I was experiencing lifted. The direction was to pray for the person you have resentment against. The Bible says the same thing: pray for your enemies and those who persecute you. This person was not a client, just an individual who overreacted about a situation and blamed me for the end result.

At the time I did not realize that I was having bitterness or anger or WHY. As I read the AA book I received a sense of freedom, because I had the courage to look at myself and **admit** that I had bitterness. No one wants to face the truth. All humans want to be accepted and loved, so when I felt **rejected and unloved** I felt hurt. The hurt would often turn to anger. I learned that, as Bob Walsh would say, every day we don't do a fourth step ("Made a searching and fearless moral inventory of ourselves") is one day closer to relapse. Although I had been doing this reflective work, I didn't know that it was in the AA book. I share this so that individuals can understand that we are always growing and learning. We must have the ongoing courage to be honest with ourselves.

I then went and talked with Paul Honess, and during our session I learned that the trigger was that I was being blamed for something I had no control over. This sense of helplessness triggered my past, and I made **a mountain out of a molehill.**

"If we say we have no sin, we deceive ourselves, and the truth is not in us. If we confess our sins, He is faithful and just to forgive us our sins and to cleanse us from all unrighteousness" (I John 1:8-9).

I worked mainly with men, doing group therapy as well as education groups. I loved my job; I taught from the heart and I understood my clients' struggles.

After Phyllis got a promotion I ended up working with the women. We used Dr. Stanton Samenow's book *Inside the Criminal Mind.* The material is awesome; it is all about the thinking. I understood that, because God changes our thinking. He tells us **what** to think to renew our minds. "Whatever is true, whatever is honorable, whatever is just, whatever is pure, whatever is lovely, whatever is commendable . . . think about these things" (Philippians 4:8).

2005, Death of the Major Lie

In order to become a New York State Credentialed Alcoholism and Substance Abuse Counselor (CASAC), one must complete coursework, hours in the field, and then the written test. After passing the written test, we were then required to present a case before the board. There was a lot to obtaining this certification.

James Holloman, Dawn Greene, and I were studying for our state test. The first part is the written exam, and I was getting nervous. Now, while in school I was allowed extra time on exams, but as I said I did not **use** that time due to the way exams were done in grad school. However, in order to obtain my M.S., I had to take the comprehensives, a national exam that is timed. I chose to take the exam in a separate location and with the extra time that I was given, due to my LD and anxiety diagnosis. I never use the extra time; I just need to know that it is there.

This test was also very important to me and I was experiencing a tremendous amount of anxiety; therefore I knew that I had to advocate for myself and let the state know that I had a right to be allowed special accommodations—separate location and extra time. The fact that the time is there allows me to calm down; being on the spot would always make the anxiety flair up.

I didn't want my peers to know that I had learning disabilities and was ashamed and embarrassed, but I had to let James know because he was going to ride with me to Rochester to take the exam. One day James and I sat in a counseling room, studying.

"James, I have to tell you that I have a learning disability and when we go to Rochester I'll get extra time to complete my test." I began to break down and cry.

James stated, "That's fine, it's your car. Take as long as you need to."

I began to sob.

James asked, "Why are you upset?"

"Well, 'cause I'm so stupid" (sobbing).

"WHAT!?"

Again, I said, "I'm so stupid."

James asked, "As evidenced by WHAT?"

"I have disabilities and I'm stupid."

"As evidenced by **WHAT?!!** . . . Oh, I know. It's by the degrees hanging in your office." He hit his head with the palm of his hand and said, "I should have known!"

"Known what?"

James said, "You **CHOOSE TO BELIEVE A LIE.** You **LIKE** to think that you're stupid."

I cry, "NO I DON'T. I JUST AM!"

"AS EVIDENCED BY WHAT?!"

"I CAN'T SPELL."

"NO, YOU **LIKE TO FEEL SORRY** FOR YOURSELF! **YOU WANT** to believe a **LIE!**"

"NO I DON'T."

"WELL THEN, why do you keep sticking your head in that toilet bowl full of shit?! You must like it!"

"No I don't" (still crying).

"Then why do you keep sticking your head in the diarrhea?"

"No, I'm not. It's the truth!"

"AS EVIDENCED BY **WHAT?!** YOUR BACHELOR'S DEGREE MAGNA CUM LAUDE?? Oh no, it must be the MASTER'S DEGREE! **That's the proof.**"

I am sobbing; I feel shame and I am vulnerable. I can't stop crying because I believe with every fiber of my being that I AM STUPID. I do believe it!!!! It's like an OLD tree with DEEP large roots that are choking the life out of me. I've always questioned every accomplishment. *Oh! The teacher likes me. That's why I got an A.*

I tell James that I think the teachers liked me and that's why I got the A's.

"Oh, is that what **they** told you?!"

No. I thought of Dr. Fiorini saying to me one night at school that I was one of the most intelligent individuals she has had the pleasure to meet. Professor DePerina said that I was an excellent candidate for a B.A. Judy Murray, another professor at OCC, said that I must pursue my master's or it would be a loss to this field. My mentor at OCC, Professor Barbara McLean, said only positive things about me. The list goes on. Emily Miller, an adjunct teacher at OCC, said wonderful things about me when she wrote a letter of recommendation for me.

"No."

"Okay, so you **like feeling stupid. You choose** to believe the **lie** and stick your head in that shit!!"

This went on for an hour. I was **broken,** and I saw that God used James Holloman to break me of the major LIE in my life.

I learned that day, almost 24 years after I had accepted Jesus Christ as my Lord and Savior, that I have a choice: to stand on the **truth** and know who I am or to believe the lie. God believes that I am worth a lot! He sent His only begotten

Son to die for me! In my place! I am His daughter. I have been bought and paid for, and I am precious to God. His Son's blood is worth more than silver or gold!!!

Now, as a clinician and a Christian, I know that **not all clients** could have received the breakthrough as I did with James's approach. **All I know is that it WORKED for me!!!**

Before this encounter, I remember at one of our staff meetings I had said that I was an idiot, and Bob Walsh got so angry with me and said firmly, "Mary, don't EVER let me hear you say that again." It was like he was protecting me from myself.

My thinking was my major problem. I was shame-based and filled with fear. When I saw the abuse and neglect from my mom and dad, I minimized it. Oh, it wasn't that bad; there weren't any bruises. In fact, it **wasn't** as bad for me as for some others, but it **was what it was,** and I had to have the courage to **face the reality** of the damage that was done, **process the pain,** and **grieve the fact** that my parents didn't love me. I had to come to accept that I did not have parents who loved me. Eventually I did accept it, and when I shared this truth with Amy Daniel, a friend from church, she said, "It was not because you were unlovable." Again, God was reiterating that what happened to me was **not** my fault. I have learned not to let the past dictate my present behaviors. I am **not** blaming my parents; they did the best they could. I am now a child of God, and I could either continue believing the lies that were ingrained into me at a very young age, or not.

Not only did I have to identify my triggers for drug use, I also had to identify what pushed my buttons. I learned that when I thought I did something wrong I would overreact and be **plagued with fear.** I remember coming home from second grade when I had failed and the fear that held me prisoner. The panic attacks that I would get when I realized that I was going to be beaten because I failed second grade! My sister Toni has always suffered trying to explain herself; she does not want to be **misunderstood!** There's a shock! She passed second grade, but Mom and Dad kept her behind so we could stay together! It makes sense that she is hyper vigilant in this area of her life.

The truth will set you free as you gain a better understanding. The truth is, I belong to Christ and He loves me and has plans for my life for good, not for evil. Perfect love casts out fear and God loves me perfectly! I use His word and I quote Scriptures when I feel fear.

The Healing Continues

From December 1997 until October 2007, I was attending the Church of the Resurrection, and my pastor was Tim Adour. He was and is a gifted preacher! He is about four years younger than me, but he was someone I looked up to.

In October 2007 he announced that he and his wife, Pastor Diana, would be leaving our church. God had called them to New York City to the Church of the Revelation in the Bronx. I was devastated. I felt all alone, abandoned.

Now what I learned from God while journaling is that I looked to Pastor Tim as a **father figure** who gave unconditional love. I **never** had that growing up from my parents. Pastor Tim was loving and approachable, and I was one of his department heads (the Sunday school superintendent). What I realized was that Pastor Tim validated me and encouraged me as a leader. It was the first time that I had a leader validate that God was using me.

I never realized before that my dad had damaged me to this deep extent. It was hard for me to let my defenses down, and because I was able to let them down with Pastor Tim I reaped the blessing of having a pastor who was trustworthy. I was not afraid of him at all.

God sent Pastor Lou Giordano to the Church of the Resurrection. One day he was preaching about prayer and talked to the fathers in the church about praying over their children and going into their rooms at night to pray. Although God has healed me, there are times when my past gets triggered and I have to allow myself to feel the pain and accept the fact that my dad was locked out of my room. I felt the pain of loss because I could not trust my own father. Around this time God continued to heal me, and when talking with an elder in the church, Bill Camloh, God continued to allow me to feel the loss of a father who could be not be trusted.

I had another significant individual leave that same year: my mentor Bob Walsh retired from Syracuse Behavioral Healthcare (SBH) in 2008. This time was different because I identified the connection right away. I knew what was going on with me emotionally.

I worked from Tuesday through Saturday with what I called the breakfast club, the Saturday crew. James, Lloyd, Joe and I were all feeling the stress with Bob gone. One Saturday James said that he was going to look for another job.

Although I loved everyone I worked with, I really couldn't see me there without James. He would call me Mini Me (i.e., mini James).

Lisa Forshee, who attended my church, had asked me on two occasions if I would be interested in working for her at Recovery Services, an outpatient treatment program. I would thank her for thinking of me but say that I was right where God wanted me at the Willows SBH inpatient program.

On Sunday, the day after James made that statement; I went to church and saw Lisa Forshee. I went over to her and asked if she was hiring. Lisa said, "YES, I'm going to put an ad in the paper." I said, "Well, I'm interested," and Lisa said, "Call me tomorrow." I called her and she told me it was 35-40 hours a week, Monday through Friday, with no on-call hours. (I was on call at the Willows every few weeks.) Then she told me the salary. I was so excited, and I called my husband Chuck at work. He said that I should do what I believed God wanted me to do. I went down to the State Tower Building and handed her my resumé. I told her about my learning disability and that my writing would need to be checked because I would need help. Lisa said that all of the staff helped each other out and that would not prevent me from getting hired.

She called me later that day and asked when I could start! I typed up my letter of resignation.

Although I knew that I would miss my colleagues at SBH, I also knew that they were a phone call away. Still, I missed Elizabeth Wright, Dina Schwartz Nisha, and Phyllis Perone more than I had anticipated.

Today I work at an outpatient treatment facility, Syracuse Recovery Services, with another great team of colleagues who support each other. I thank God that he has also given me a great, approachable boss whom I can talk to—Lisa Forshee. No matter how busy she is she STOPS to assist her team. She is an extremely gifted clinician and an excellent supervisor.

I am also running the Seeking Safety program, which was developed by Dr. Lisa Najavits. This program works with Post Traumatic Stress Disorder PTSD and substance abuse clients. Bob Walsh introduced it to me when I was working at SBH. I recommend anyone in the chemical dependence substance abuse field to check out the treatment manual. As I look back on my journey, I understand the importance of identifying what is being triggered and implementing new coping skills; the point is to **not** allow your past to dictate your present behaviors.

When I began this job in September 2008, one of my first encounters was with a former client. I had worked with him years earlier, and he was not ready for recovery at that time. When he began outpatient treatment at Recovery Services, he was asked if he minded working with me. He said he was happy to work with me: "We go way back, and I know that she doesn't sugarcoat shit. Mary will tell me straight out what I NEED to hear." I mention him because once I told him that I

218 ★ *Misery To Ministry*

was writing this book, he would encourage me every so often by asking if I was still working on it. He said he will read it, and he thinks that others also will want to hear my story. Working in this field I must be careful not to break the federal law of confidentiality. So, that does limit me when I want to mention individuals whom I have had the privilege to minister to.

One client (who I will call Linda) told me that she believes God put me in her path. I had worked with her in the past at the Willows, and the day she had her evaluation at Recovery Services she was scheduled to meet with me. When she arrived and saw me there, she knew that God had put me in her path, and I helped her to surrender to God through the Lord Jesus Christ. She attends 12-step meetings and God is ministering to her.

While working at Recovery Services, I was running a group and one of the females began to attack me verbally. It is during times like these that I see the power of God working in my life to touch others. I was able to validate and minister to her through the power of the Holy Spirit. The lady deescalated and actually listened to what I had to say. When the group ended, every lady left that room and said, "Awesome group, Mary! You ROCK!" I hear these statements often, and they are evidence that the best counselor who ever existed is working through me to help others, and that is the Holy Spirit, **the** wonderful counselor.

If you run into some of my clients, you may hear them say, "Don't get upset. This is just a test *(from your national broadcasting system)*. It is a choice to yield either to the old flesh—I call mine the brat Mary—or to the Spirit. Most times you can change your mood if you begin to be thankful.

I tell my clients to ask their higher power for a Holy Spirit tranquilizer.

I know that I am not the only therapist who asks, "Who is renting space in your head?" I ask, "DID YOU COLLECT THE RENT MONEY?!! IF NOT, THEN YOU MUST EVICT THAT

THING OR PERSON FROM YOUR THOUGHTS, and then go on to the serenity prayer."

And when the diseases try to **punk them,** as Bob Walsh would say, I tell them to say, "TALK TO THE HAND! I'VE BEEN THERE, DONE THAT, AND I HAVE THE T-SHIRT!!! NOT ME, NOT NOW!!!" Change = Recovery. If getting angry at the disease helps, go for it!

After 29 years of walking with my Lord and Savior, I still have a lot of work to do to become who God wants me to be.

I say to everyone who reads this book, always be open to learn, because despite my ability to survive, I know that we need to go deeper and heal, process grief, and accept. Pushing down, minimizing will never produce growth.

I also say to all clinicians who read this "we all must face our own demons in order to help our clients."

May all who read this find hope in the Lord Jesus Christ as you continue on your journey while here on earth.

If I do not get the joy of meeting you here on earth, I will see you on the other side. May God richly bless you.

Acknowledgments

I want to thank God first and then my husband Chuck, and my sister Toni; the hours that they spent reading and re-reading this manuscript seemed endless. It's because of their dedication and the constant encouragement they gave me that this project was completed; without them, I do not think that I could have endured the emotional stress that came with this endeavor. I also want to acknowledge one of my closest friends, Beth Levernosh, who spent hours reading this manuscript. She not only provided me with priceless feedback, she was a constant encourager to me from the moment I told her that I was going to write my memoir.

I want to personally thank Tim Bennett for helping me with this project. It was after meeting with Tim on July 25, 2009 that the dream of this book became a reality. I knew that he had the experience and the associations that would allow him to help me. Publishing was definitely uncharted waters for me. I am grateful to Tim for navigating this endeavor to its completion.

Although I do not know how to contact Gloria, I thank her for her obedience to God. She followed His direction when he "pressed me on her heart" and because of her obedience to God my life changed.

I also want to acknowledge the professors at Onondaga Community College who encouraged me to continue with my education. Also, I'm grateful to the professors at Oswego State University for equipping me with the skills necessary to be the clinician that I am today.

I thank Andrea, the counselor at Oswego who finally helped me to process and grieve the loss of never having loving parents, never feeling loved, and never being that special, precious little girl to Mom or Dad.

There are so many people who have touched my life in positive ways that I could not name you all; but know that the positive acts of love and kindness that you have given me have not been taken for granted. God has used them in my life. God bless and thank you.

What Happened to John?

In his own words, John answers that question.

M Y NAME IS John Haupt and WOW I've come a long way. My famous quote I put in my high school book is "Life is a mystery to be lived, and not a problem to be solved." I like to start off by saying I am grateful to be where I am at this period of time. I can see my whole life behind me, and that's what I call amazing. To get to this point, it was a rough experience pertaining to my early childhood years. Before I go any further I want to point out that I have no negative thoughts toward my parents. Despite the fact that many have had a bad childhood, we should never take it out on the present. Never say to your children, "This is the way I was brought up; it is my way." Leave the past behind and show your family true love. My parents never showed me the right way. It was childhood abuse, but I can live with it, and as I said before I have no hate in my heart toward them. Up until the age of 9 years old I used to get beaten with a paddle almost every week. Remember those paddles with the ball on them? My dad would buy a new one, and every time he bought one he would take the ball off and scar my behind till it got blistered red. Most of the time I was beaten for no reason at all. Right around that time in my life I had a massive nervous breakdown. I was sent to Kings Park State Mental Hospital, Kings Park Long Island.

Kings Park Psychiatric Center was at one time the world's largest hospital. It opened its doors in 1887 and closed in 1996. If you go to their web site, the information provided will show you that Kings Park has made its mark in history; it is now a historic landmark. When I first looked at their web site, the first thing that popped up was the building I stayed in. I enlarged the photo and it dawned on me: I was looking at the exact room that I stayed in for two years. This was back in the heyday in 1962. As I look back it's incredible; I can see myself at 9 years old in that window looking down towards the park and sidewalks. I stayed on the 5th floor, the first window next to the arch. All of the windows had steel bars on the outside. As I looked at this web site I was flooded with memories, things that I have not thought about in decades. When I saw the windows on the 9th floor, all of a sudden I remembered. I used to go up to the 9th floor ward along with several kids to clean the rooms about twice a week. I went to the exact room four stories above my room to clean that room first, and I would always look out that window for a brief period. Being four flights higher and having the same view made me feel as if I was up really high. The upper floors had very sick, chronic patients that couldn't perform everyday chores. We also cleaned their recreation rooms, called day rooms. Our day rooms were very large, but the upper level day rooms were half the size of the one that I used. The day rooms all had a television in a corner on the top shelf, chained so nobody could mess with it. There were about five adults who watched and monitored everything we did in the day room. No one was allowed to touch the dials on the television except them. We used to sit in a very large group on the floor to watch television.

I have a scar on my chin; it took place in the day room. I was being spun around by my feet, almost like a helicopter blade. The fun ended when my feet were no longer being held by two hands. I flew in the air briefly, and then fell onto the waxed floor; I slid until I hit the radiator chin first. I now have a Kings Park Landmark scar on my chin.

At Kings Park State Hospital I was also introduced to the white straight jacket. It covered the upper body down to the waistline. Both arms looped around each other and were tied very tight. I felt like I was hugging myself; there were times when I had to keep it on all day. Putting on restraint to put the jacket on was the tough part. You can imagine how wild I became under this condition, like any kid would. Back in the 1960s restraints and straight jackets were always used. The day room also had its share of fist fights, which I did sometime get into. I won some and lost some, and for every action there is a reaction. Anyone who got into trouble had to face the penalty; you would be put in a straight jacket and sent to your bedroom, locked up for the whole day. The only reprieve was when you would be untied briefly so you could eat your meals under supervision. Today restraints are required only as a last resort. The beating of the paddle and, I forgot to mention, the belt and buckle were the reasons I ended up here.

Now let's talk about another picture that brings back memories: the long hallway that ran along our steel door bedrooms. Every night we sat along the hallway before bedtime. We would get generic government bread—four slices with peanut butter and jelly. Sometimes we would get graham crackers, and to top it off, a steel glass of milk. All of these items came in a firm plastic wrap with no logo on the outside of the wrappers. All of our meals were eaten on, believe it or not, steel prison trays. During the summer season we would get on a bus a couple times a week and go down to the beach and swim. We only stayed for about an hour. The day room, the playground, my bedroom, and thorazine, 500 mg twice a day, were my life at Kings Park State Hospital. Looking out of my bedroom window I thought there was hope, as I saw people walking about.

After two years at Kings Park I went to Children's Village in Dobbs Ferry, N.Y. At this boarding school I was taught how to grow up and face the world. In my high school years I was in a boys home in Nyack, N.Y. I graduated from Nyack High and moved to Flushing in Queens, N.Y., and there I began announcer training studios and went into radio broadcasting.

My first job was in Augusta, Georgia at WRDWA James Brown radio station. I met James several times when he came to town. He was always on the road with his band. His music will always live on. After I left Augusta I worked in Savannah for a while, then ended my radio trail in Jacksonville, Florida at WPDW radio. After radio, I joined the Marines and traveled the Pacific coast from 1976 to 1979. I have lived in Syracuse ever since. I worked in a milk plant for 14 years and did some more radio in Syracuse. Radio here was so much fun, especially working alongside Dr. Rick Wright. We used to talk about James Brown so much it was a natural part of the day. At present I am working at St Joseph's Hospital in Syracuse, N.Y.

I can get access to my personal files if I want, but I choose to keep them concealed in Kings Park Landmark vault. As they say, case closed. I am good to go. When asked now how I feel about my past, my response is that I am grateful I was able to get help. I have seen it all, from home abuse, mental breakdown, hospital, and boarding school to group home. Finally, my world is in a forward direction. The afterlife of being an adult has all become a big crossword puzzle. It is a matter of connecting the right pieces together. My message is to never give up no matter what. Show 100% love toward your children, family, and everyone around you. If you suspect someone is being abused, there is help. Back in the 1960s there were no cell phones or home computers. Today, help is just a fingertip away. Remember, never say: "This is the way my parents brought me up," especially if you were a victim of child abuse. In closing, please remember that love begins at the home first. I have to thank God for bringing me through. He is an amazing God and He will hear your cry.

Appendix

WHO AM I IN CHRIST　　　　　*compiler unknown*

I Am Accepted

John 1:12	*I am God's child.*
John 15:15	*I am Christ's friend.*
Romans 5:1	*I have been justified.*
1 Corinthians 6:17	*I am united with the Lord, and I am one spirit with Him.*
1 Corinthians 6:20	*I have been bought with a price. I belong to God.*
1 Corinthians 12:27	*I am a member of Christ's Body.*
Ephesians 1:1	*I am a saint.*
Ephesians 1:5	*I have been adopted as God's child.*
Ephesians 2:18	*I have direct access to God through the Holy Spirit.*
Colossians 1:14	*I have been redeemed and forgiven of all my sins.*
Colossians 2:10	*I am complete in Christ.*

I Am Secure

Romans 8:1-2	*I am free from condemnation.*
Romans 8:28	*I am assured that all things work together for good.*
Romans 8:31-34	*I am free from any condemning charges against me.*
Romans 8:35-39	*I cannot be separated from the love of God.*
2 Corinthians 1:21-22	*I have been established, anointed and sealed by God.*
Philippians 1:6	*I am confident that the good work God has begun in me will be perfected.*

Philippians 3:20	*I am a citizen of heaven.*
Colossians 3:3	*I am hidden with Christ in God.*
2 Timothy 1:7	*I have not been given a spirit of fear, but of power, love and a sound mind.*
Hebrews 4:16	*I can find grace and mercy in time of need.*
1 John 5:18	*I am born of God and the evil one cannot touch me.*

I Am Significant

Matthew 5:13-14	*I am the salt and light of the earth.*
John 15:1,5	*I am a branch of the true vine, a channel of His life.*
John 15:16	*I have been chosen and appointed to bear fruit.*
Acts 1:8	*I am a personal witness of Christ.*
1 Corinthians 3:16	*I am God's temple.*
2 Corinthians 5:17-21	*I am a minister of reconciliation for God.*
2 Corinthians 6:1	*I am God's coworker (see 1 Corinthians 3:9).*
Ephesians 2:6	*I am seated with Christ in the heavenly realm.*
Ephesians 2:10	*I am God's workmanship.*
Ephesians 3:12	*I may approach God with freedom and confidence.*
Philippians 4:13	*I can do all things through Christ who strengthens me.*

FAITH CONFESSIONS
by Monica D. Johns

A: He has made me ACCEPTED in the Beloved.

B: He has BLESSED me with every spiritual blessing in the heavenly places in Christ.

C: I have been CREATED in Christ Jesus to do good works. I am COMPLETE in Him.

D: The Lord DELIGHTS in me. He is causing me to walk out His plan for me.

E: The Holy Spirit ENJOYS living within me! The Holy Spirit is EAGER to commune with me!

F: I am FREE in Christ FOREVER! FOREVER starts right now! I do not have to be FORMAL with Him, because He is my FRIEND and I am His FRIEND.

G: His GRACE toward me is infinite and His GRACE covers every conceivable thing in my life whether it is past, present, or future. His GRACE is permanent and eternal. He loves to make all GRACE abound toward me and He makes sure that I have all I need for every GOOD work.

H: The HOLY Spirit testifies that I am God's child. He has made me HOLY because I am in Him and He is in me. There is no question about this and there is no need to second-guess this.

I: He lives INSIDE of me and He has reproduced Himself in me. Now He is patiently causing me to walk out His plan and is reproducing His character in me. I can rely on Him completely without having a sense of neediness because He is my provision.

J: I am not under any JUDGMENT whatsoever. There is no JUDGMENT of me because the Lord Jesus Christ took care of everything at Calvary. Furthermore, He does not give any one the right to JUDGE me. Therefore, I can live free of people's opinions.

K: The KINGDOM of God is within me. He has made me a KING and a priest for Himself.

L: He LOVES me and He really LIKES me too! He LOVES it when I talk with Him.

M: God has not given me a spirit of fear, but of power, of love, and of a sound MIND. He has angels, MINISTERING spirits, sent to MINISTER to my needs because I am one who will inherit salvation.

N: He supplies all of my NEEDS according to His riches in glory by Christ Jesus.

O: He is the one who ORDAINS every OUTCOME. He is OVER every circumstance, situation, authority, person, and organization. Therefore, He OVERSEES every aspect of my life.

P: God is my PEACE. He works in me causing me to will and to act according to His good PURPOSE.

Q: He does not mind when I QUESTION Him about things.

R: I am free to RELATE to God based on His RIGHTEOUS-NESS, which He has freely given to me.

S: I STAND fast in the liberty wherewith Christ has made me free, and I do not allow anyone to entangle me with a yoke of bondage.

T: He TRANSFORMS my THOUGHTS so that they line up with His TRUTH. He is TRUSTWORTHY. I can TRUST Him to bring His will to pass in my life.

U: I can rest in the knowledge that every aspect of my life is UNDER His Blood.

continued . . .

V: He has already delivered the VICTORY to me.

W: All things WORK together for my good because I am called according to His purpose. He is causing me to WALK out His plan for me.

X: I can allow Him to X-RAY my life and reveal things to me without being afraid.

Y: He YEARNS for my companionship and I YEARN for His companionship.

Z: How many things can separate me from Him: ZERO! How many ways does He love me and want to bless me: a ZILLION.

© *2010 Monica D. Johns (used with permission)*

Brad
salt city

Breinigsville, PA USA
07 March 2011
257043BV00001B/4/P